Discovering
Paris Bistros

Gaston Wijnen

Translated from the original Dutch by the author

ROSENDALE PRESS

To the memory of Jean-Pierre Imbach with all my gratitude for giving me the inspiration to write this guide and for countless invaluable tips and advice on improvements; and to Robert Courtine who keeps my love of Paris alive with his weekly gastronomic essays in **Le Monde.**

Cover design by Robert Budwig
Maps by Alistair Powell
Typeset by Chiltern Publishing, Beaconsfield, Bucks
Printed in Great Britain by Cromwell Press, Melksham, Wilts

ISBN 1 872803 00 8

Discovering
Paris Bistros

Publisher's Note

This guide to the neighbourhood bistros of Paris has grown out of the earlier *Paris Gourmand* by Jean-Pierre Imbach. For some time his friend, Gaston Wijnen, took up the knife and fork as his collaborator and for the last five years this guide to Paris bistros has appeared on the continent under Gaston Wijnen's name alone.

In this first English language edition, new and up-to-date for 1991, the visitor to Paris will find descriptions of new discoveries as well as the traditional and indestructible old places that best meet the exacting standards of Parisians in their daily appreciation of good food and good value. Frequented by the French rather than by tourists, these are *les bonnes adresses,* all the visitor really needs to join in one of the best strands of the gastronomic life of the city.

Contents

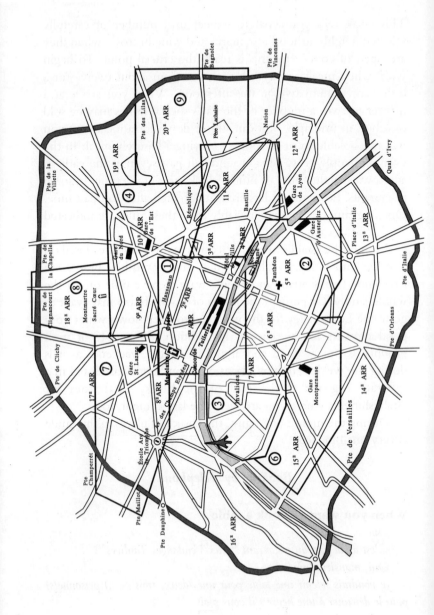

How to use this Guide

This book tells you what to expect in a number of carefully selected neighbourhood restaurants and wine bistros – when they are open of course, for this is really the crucial point. To begin with, when meals are served: these are from about twelve (or a little earlier) until two in the afternoon. When you arrive at a quarter to two, a number of the day's special dishes may be sold out, but, in principle, you can still sit down for a meal. But you will not be able to sit for hours enjoying a leisurely meal. In the evening people go to dine around half past seven at the earliest, and toward eight-thirty or nine o'clock most of the time. In some restaurants, however, orders are not accepted after half past nine. Opening times varying appreciably from these rules are indicated at the end of each article.

Most of the establishments described in this guide are closed on Sundays and holidays. That is quite understandable; bistros are frequently family affairs and people want to have time off for the whole family. Or perhaps the *patron* of a wine bistro may want to go to the Loire valley for the weekend to track down wines from good growers for his clients. In addition, the supply of fresh produce is not as good and abundant during weekends as it is during the week. The few places open on Sunday are listed in a separate register at the end of the book. That goes for establishments where you are welcome late at night, too.

During the month of August, the choice of places in this guide is very small indeed.

Booking by Telephone

When you want to book a table

Oui . . . Allo . . .

C'est de la part du restaurant "Aux Vendanges Tardives"?

Oui, monsieur/madame . . .

Je voudrais retenir une table pour une (deux, trois . . .) personne(s) pour le déjeuner à une heure s'il vous plaît.

or

Je voudrais retenir une table pour une (deux, trois . . .) personne(s) pour ce soir à huit heures et demie s'il vous plaît.

Ah, je suis désolé(e), monsieur/madame, nous sommes complets à midi/ce soir.

Ah, c'est dommage. Merci quand même. Au revoir, monsieur/madame.

Au revoir, monsieur/madame . . . click.

or

Bien sûr, monsieur/madame, quel est votre nom, s'il vous plaît?

Je m'appelle Green.

Voulez vous épeler, s'il vous plaît, monsieur/madame?

Bien sûr, c'est G.r.e.e.n.

Merci bien, monsieur/madame, et à toute à l'heure/et à ce soir!

When you want to know whether a restaurant is open

Voici le restaurant "La Vache Qui Rit" . . . Allo . . . j'écoute . . .

Vous êtes ouvert pour le déjeuner/le dîner, monsieur/madame?

Bien sûr, monsieur/madame!

Ah, ça convient, on pourrait donc aller chez vous aujourd'hui.

Merci bien, monsieur/madame et au revoir!

Au revoir, monsieur/madame! . . . click.

The best way to call from a public telephone booth in Paris is by means of a *télécarte*. It is cheaper and the *télécarte* phone booths are less frequently out of order. *Télécartes* can be bought at any post office and cost about 50F for 50 units and 115F for 120 units.

If you do not get an answer before 11 am or between three and six in the afternoon, that does not necessarily mean that the restaurant is closed. Simply try again half an hour later. When you have booked a table, do arrive precisely at the time you have booked (not more than five minutes late) and do not forget to call when, unexpectedly, you cannot show up on time or at all.

There is an amusing anecdote about a Paris restaurant owner and one of his clients. The client had booked a table by telephone but did not show up; he did not cancel either. At three o'clock in the morning, the *patron* called his client asking urgently whether he could now let the cook go home.

Price Guide

The approximate price given at the end of each article concerns the total price of a complete meal (including entrée, main dish, cheese, or dessert) with wine and a cup of coffee. In the case of the wine bistros, indicated by a wine glass, this is a little different: here, the price tells you how much one or two glasses of wine and a cold or warm snack may cost you without necessarily being supplemented by an entrée, a dessert and a cup of coffee.

I have visited each establishment in this guide at least once and paid my bills from my own pocket. Most of the time I left just as anonymously as I had come in and the majority of the restaurateurs and *bistrotiers* knew nothing about my intention of writing this guidebook. I have very seldom taken the cheapest dish or the lowest-priced wine and the prices I give are not minimum prices, but rather recommendations: this is the amount you can reasonably spend here, you will then have eaten and drunk well, as well as is possible in this establishment without having to feel afterwards that you have spent too much.

It can occur therefore that the price shown alongside a more expensive restaurant can be lower than for a place that is asking lower prices on the whole but where everything is really worth while and excellent value for money.

Of course I cannot guarantee that the prices quoted will remain stable, because rents, energy costs, the prices of goods and taxes have an irresistible tendency to go upward, trailing restaurant (and other) prices in their wake. The rise in prices has been an average 10 to 15 per cent per year over the last five years. If you should encounter changes out of all proportion, I would appreciate it very much if you would notify me. That is also the case if you find a restaurant disappointing. Often a change of ownership or of the chef is sufficient to change a good address into a bad one. At the end of this book there is a request for comments and suggestions about other restaurants that might be included. Your co-operation remains an essential element of the continual growth and improvement of this guide as the numerous reactions from my continental readers have shown since 1985. I shall research your suggestions with pleasure. Thank you for your help.

Gaston Wijnen

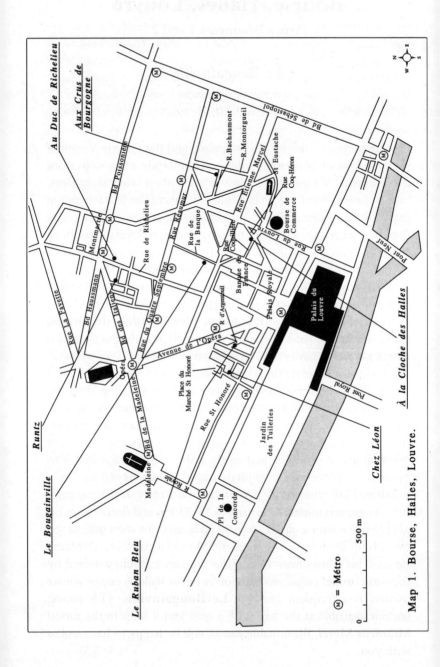

Map 1. Bourse, Halles, Louvre.

Bourse, Halles, Louvre

Arrondissements 1 and 2

Le Bougainville

5 rue de la Banque
Tel: 42.60.05.19

On the corner of the rue de la Banque and the Galerie Vivienne with its array of interesting little shops, and only a few steps from the premises of one of the most reputed Paris wine merchants, Lucien Legrand at 1 rue de la Banque, is one of the few remaining genuine Paris bistros of authentic simplicity. It welcomes a steady flow of regulars (who have their own personal red and white check cotton napkins) as well as less regular visitors from other parts of Paris (and abroad) every weekday around noon.

Le Bougainville, named after the French navigator Antoine de Bougainville who died in this building on 31st August 1811, celebrated its twenty-fifth anniversary in 1988. Its prices, characteristically, have only gone up very slightly during the seven years in which I have come to know it.

The décor is purely functional: formica tables with paper cloths and napkins, and pale neon lighting from the ceiling. But the atmosphere is cheerfully engaging and the clientèle very mixed. The undeniable charm of the place easily overcomes such trifles as the impression that the hurried waitress wants you to bark out your order almost as promptly and curtly as she will then transmit it to kitchen and counter, simultaneously jotting it down on a numbered bill which she places under the ashtray. If you are early (they begin serving meals as early as 11.30 am, and don't count on getting a seat after a quarter to one), you may not want to miss the pleasure of a cool glass of excellent Muscadet de Sèvre-et-Maine *sur lie*. This comes from one of the growers carefully selected by the good broker (*négociant*) Sauvion et Fils at Vallet – one of whose owners is a frequent guest of **Le Bougainville**. This young wine is available at the bar at 5F a glass and if he is in the mood Monsieur Morel, the amiable *patron*, will be happy to have a glass with you.

There is no fixed-price menu, but the prices are friendly, the portions generous, almost abundant. The *saucisson de montagne* (slices of air-dried sausage), the *andouille de Vire* (thin slices of smoked, tripe-filled sausage from Normandy), the *terrine d'Auvergne*, and the *rillettes de Sarthe* (finely chopped pork slowly simmered in its own fat) are available for 7.50F to 8F. *Crudités* (assorted raw vegetables) are 9.50F, and the *jambon de pays d'Aoste* (uncooked mountain ham), the most expensive entrée, costs 25F. There are always two main dishes which change every day: for instance, leg of lamb with flageolet beans or sautéed potatoes (*gigot d'agneau* – 42F) and *petit salé aux lentilles* (salt pork with lots of steaming hot, flavoursome lentils – 42F). There is always fish on Fridays. A steady item on the bill of fare is the steak at 35F. Cantal, Gruyére, and Camembert are the cheese options at 7.50F.

The delicious home-made fruit tarts at **Le Bougainville** – on my last visit a thin apple tart, whose flavour was as exquisite as its appearance (a rare occurrence in the Paris of the Nineties, alas) – are better than in many other establishments and many times less expensive: 10F. For instance, the nearby **Vaudeville**, a link in the chain of establishments to which **Terminus Nord** (see p.91) belongs, charges 33F for an item of less allure and personality . . . but then they are large and fashionable.

The carafe of house red wine costs 9.50F for three quarters of a litre (40cl: 6.50F; 22cl: 4.50F). I had a smooth and pleasant Côtes-du-Rhône from the Cave de la Vigneronne at Valledieu-Buisson for 30F a half-bottle (45F the bottle). There is also a Cahors, an earthy red from the south-west, for 75F.

There is no obligation here to have a full three-course meal, but you can inexpensively add on a side dish of green salad (7.50F). I find it difficult to forego an entrée of good *charcuterie* – sometimes they have *rillons*, cubes of pork cooked until crisp, a speciality from the lower Loire valley (Touraine, Anjou). And I never like to miss the fabulous fruit cake. A small cup of coffee costs 4.50F.

Open: *Meals served from 11.30 am*
Closed: *Every night and Sunday all day*
Métro: *3 Bourse ; 7 Pyramides*   **Map:** *1*
Approximate price: *80 F*

A la Cloche des Halles
28 rue Coquillière
Tel: 42.36.93.89

This is a wine bistro in the old authentic vein, right in the centre of Paris, in the area where the famous Halles, the central market providing fresh produce for Paris, had been located until it moved to Rungis, about twenty kilometres south, in 1968; since then it has been replaced by a spectacular shopping centre, the Forum des Halles, the Pompidou Building and other tourist attractions. This unexpected oasis of authenticity contrasts with the rather expensive wine bars operated by immigrant English that have sprouted here during the past ten to twenty years.

It was Gaston Balancin of the excellent wine bistro **Chez Gaston**, in the old Marais district (see p. 103) who drew my attention to **A la Cloche des Halles**. And the first sip of their 1988 Mâcon blanc (7.50F per 8cl, 15F per 15cl, 70F the bottle) at the shiny brass *zinc* at the corner of the rue Coq-Héron and the rue Coquillière halfway between the Banque de France and the Bourse de Commerce confirmed my first impression: the wine was as unadulterated, excellent and authentic as this old bistro with its real bell (*la cloche*) mounted on the outside wall.

Serge Lesage, the owner of this fine specimen of a Parisian wine bistro, had been awarded the *meilleur pot* award in 1986 in recognition of his outstanding merits: the originality and authenticity of his wines (bought directly from the wine growers and bottled by himself), his bread, cheese and *charcuterie*, sausages, hams, terrines and pâtés.

Let me cite a few examples of the wines available at **La Cloche** when I visited it. The cheapest is a simple, fresh white Cheverny, a V.D.Q.S. from the Touraine region for 5.50F a small glass (11F for the 15cl glass and 55F the bottle). The white 1988 Burgundy of the proprietors Michel Mallard et Fils at Ladoix-Serrigny near Beaune (8cl: 8.50F; 15cl: 17F) had an authentic fragrance, was served at an appropriately cool temperature, and its degree of acidity seemed just right, although to my taste it exhibited less character than the Mâcon. The 1988 Bourgeuil, a red Loire wine with an old and present-day reputation (6.50F and 13F) had considerable body but was rather one-dimensional and, like the 1989 Côte-de-Brouilly, one of the better *crus* of the Beaujolais region, was served at a temperature which is just too warm for these young, light red wines. But if you get there before three o'clock in the afternoon you have more of a chance of finding these red wines at a sufficiently cool temperature, a member of the staff who has worked in **La Cloche** for more than seventeen years explained to me. Maybe this has something to do with the refrigerators not yet having been opened too many times. Other Beaujolais *crus* available: Morgon, Chiroubles, Fleurie, Juliénas, all of them for about one franc per centilitre. An occasion to sample them all!

As in almost all Parisian cafés, there is a surcharge if you prefer to sit down on an elegantly-shaped black Thonet chair at one of the small, round tables sparsely placed along the walls of the small bistro, or in a small room behind the bar, or again outside on the tiny pavement terrace. But at **La Cloche** you only pay a modest 50 centimes or 1F more on each small or average glass of wine. And the *tartines* (slices of wholesome sourdough bread from the baker Manzagol, a former employee of the famous Paris baker Poilâne) with ham cut from the bone (*jambon à l'os*) or raw ham (*cru*) or Mâcon sausage (*saucisson du Mâconnais*) costs 13F to 15F at the counter, or 16F to 18F sitting down. Very reasonable considering that there are lots of cafés in Paris where you pay one and a half times to twice as much once at a table. The platters (*assiettes*) of ham or mixed *charcuterie* are 32F and 35F respectively, no matter where you have them served. There is no surcharge on the cheese platter either (Crottin de Chèvre (goat), Brie de Meaux, Cantal, Camembert, Pont l'Evêque . . . 40F for one, 50F for two persons). Any of the cheeses available can be ordered separately at 17F or 18F. Ah, and they make their own *jambon persillé* (ham in white wine jelly with parsley) here (25F).

Lots of real wine lovers visit regularly, a fact which inspires confidence and provides jolly good company too! But the omelette (for around 15F) and cup of tea that a solitary girl was ordering for herself poses no problem and produces no raised eyebrows. There is even beer on draught although a faded cardboard sign on the door says in bold green letters *"Ici on boit du* vin!!!" (One drinks wine here!!!), a recommendation I strongly subscribe to. But then you can always order a caramelised apple pie (*tarte Tatin*), a *clafoutis* (fruit in batter) or a fruit cake for around 20F with or without a cup of coffee (4F at the counter) as an alternative to the wine-bread-ham-sausage-cheese option – or to finish it off.

Open: *8 am to 9 pm; Saturday 10 am to 5 pm*
Closed: *Saturday night; all day Sunday*
Métro: *1 Louvre*   **Map:** *1*
Approximate price: *75F*
No reservations

Aux Crus de Bourgogne
3 rue Bachaumont
Tel: 42.33.48.24

The rue Bachaumont is a quiet side-street off the lively rue Montorgeuil with its bustling street-market, where a number of local restaurateurs shop for their supplies. Behind a wide brown façade with lots of window panes, the world of Paris at the turn of the last century opens up for you. According to Francis Bouvier, the grandson of the legendary original *patronne*, Madame Larcier, who died in 1987, none of the décor has changed since the family took over the restaurant in 1930. An oasis of nostalgia! On the stately buffet-counter of solid black wood there is room for a few green plants and, sometimes, a large black cat answering to the name of Zorro. Left of the entrance there is a display of fresh *langoustes* (crayfish), a house speciality which, served with mayonnaise at the incredibly low price of 75F, attracts a daily flow of enthusiasts from all over Paris, as does the *foie gras d'oie frais* at the same price.

There is room for about seventy people at tables covered with red and white check tablecloths and napkins, between large green plants and gigantic mirrors on the walls, but I strongly recommend booking for lunch or dinner. After nine-thirty in the evening it is impossible to find a table otherwise.

I could not resist the temptation to treat myself to a portion of *foie gras* which, according to the *cognoscenti*, is even better here than in many a reputedly great restaurant where the price is twice or three times as high. This elegant dish, accompanied by a small glass of sweet Sauternes (30F), was followed by a tasty medium-sized, well-filled plate of enticingly scented and very savoury lean breast of duck with perfectly cooked tagliatelle, then the most expensive item on the menu. On a more recent occasion, I had a modest and very correct *jambon persillé de Bourgogne* (ham in a white wine and parsley jelly) at 50F and an excellent *panaché de lotte et saumon haricots verts* (ragout of monk fish and salmon with French beans) for 120F, now, next to the *filet de boeuf béarnaise haricots verts* (fillet of beef) for 150F, the most expensive dish on the menu.

A standard dish at **Aux Crus de Bourgogne** is still the classic *coq au brouilly* (chicken in red wine) for 90F while the Brouilly wine itself, one of the better *crus* of the Beaujolais region, which was very good a few years ago (1986), is now less attractive and frankly too expensive at 120F; an Anjou *rouge*, a full-bodied fresh red wine with a certain distinction and character, is a better choice at 80F a bottle. Don't overlook the *côtes d'agneau grillées* (lamb chops) with *haricots verts* at 85F which is much appreciated here.

For dessert I took the *mille-feuilles* (puff pastry) at 40F because I was disappointed to learn from the waitress that the *clafoutis aux fruits de saison* (fruit batter pudding – 35F) was not made with cherries, as the classical recipe and the season prescribe (we were in June, after all), but with *mirabelles* (yellow plums). There is chocolate cake, lemon cake, ice cream and sorbets: all around 35F. Coffee is 10F.

You can choose a complete meal – starting with *salade au noix* (with walnuts) 30F, the lamb chops, a cheese platter for 41F, and a fine bottle of Anjou *rouge* plus coffee – and your bill will not exceed 250F. Not a bad buy for a good meal in *le vrai vieux Paris*!

Open: *Orders taken until 11 pm,* foie gras *and* langouste *until 11.30 pm*
Closed: *Saturday; Sunday*
Métro: *3 Sentier or 4, 7, 13 Les Halles*   **Map:** *1*
Approximate price: *250F*

Au Duc de Richelieu
110 rue de Richelieu
Tel: 42.96.38.38

One Saturday I dedicated to the **Duc de Richelieu**. What was to be a simple and hearty bistro meal – a different classic *plat du jour* is presented every day – became a very special wine adventure.

But before relating this, I want to run through the regular fare: *coq au vin* (chicken in red wine), *boeuf bourguignon* (beef stew), *pot-au-feu, foie purée* (calf's liver with mashed potatoes) are a few examples of a particular day's special dish all priced at about 60F, good French home cooking (*cuisine ménagère* or *bourgeoise*), which daily attract journalists from the local newspaper offices, clerks and directors from the neighbouring banks, and local inhabitants; in short, a heterogenous crowd which forms a large and lively company intermingling with the help of a steady flow of good Beaujolais in their glasses, brought up from the cellars at the rate of over three hundred bottles a day. And all this wine, it cannot be emphasised strongly enough, comes directly from the growers where Monsieur Georgé, the *patron*, has been sampling, selecting and buying for more than thirty years. But Monsieur Georgé does more: he does not just buy and sell his wines, he is carefully ageing them as well. Right here in the middle of Paris!

While waiting for my companions at the copper *zinc*, next to an elegant lady sitting on a bar stool eating the day's special dish *pintade au chou* (guinea fowl and cabbage), and hearty sourdough bread from the famous Paris baker Poilâne (8 rue du Cherche-Midi, 6th *arrondissement*), I start to sample some of the wines listed on the blackboard.

The uncontested star of the establishment is the Fleurie, light and full of flavour with a very persistent finale. It costs 11F or 22F per glass of 8cl or 15cl contents; a bottle costs 110F and a half-bottle 56F at the table. I rather fancied the 1989 Regnié on my last visit (8.50F/17F per glass) which was fresh, concentrated and clearly exhibited the cherry-and-kirsch flavour so characteristic of this Beaujolais *cru,* a neighbour of the illustrious Morgon. The Chiroubles for the same price is smooth, charming, almost feminine and has a subtle bitter note in the finale. There is also a Chénas which is perhaps the least interesting of the *crus* available here, while the Beaujolais *blanc* (8.50F/17F per glass) is full-bodied and harmonious. Other white wines on the board: a young Muscadet de Sèvre-et-Maine *sur lie* at 5.20F/10.40F and an ordinary Muscadet, the cheapest wine on offer, for 4.30F/8.50F. The cheapest red is a Côtes-du-Rhône for 5F/10F

A simple snack is always available. A *tartine* (open sandwich) with *rillettes d'oie* (minced pork and goose meat cooked in fat) costs 11.50F at the *zinc*, while a *tartine* with raw air-dried country ham *(jambon de pays)* is 17F including a supplement of 4F for butter and Poilâne bread (instead of ordinary white French bread).

My company had arrived, so it was time to go to our table! We had booked in the morning, which is strictly necessary here even on Saturday. In a small corner the three of us just about managed to squeeze in around a square wooden table. We started with the *rillettes d'oie* (24F), served in a brown earthenware pot, a spicy *terrine d'Auvergne* (22F) and a few slices of raw country ham (30F), accompanied by a half-bottle of Fleurie. Willem chose the *pintade au chou* (guinea fowl with cabbage) while the young lady and I shared a *côte de boeuf* for two (190F) which turned out to be a gigantic, succulent and firm roast rib of beef that we did not manage to finish completely despite our healthy appetites! There is a 1976(!) Fleurie available, aged for more than ten years in Monsieur Georgé's cellar, a very rare event because, like all Beaujolais wines (except Morgon and Moulin-à-Vent from good years) Fleurie normally does not improve with age and can become flat and insipid. But Paul Goergé's 1976 Fleurie exhaled a deep complex aroma, complemented by a fully developed flavour which made me think of a ripe Burgundy rather than of a fresh flowery Fleurie. The difference between the Gamay grape's typical flavour and that of a Burgundy's Pinot Noir seemed completely effaced. I had started by sampling the vintage Fleurie already open at the *zinc* after spotting it on the board. At the table it turned out that the wine needed about ten minutes to develop its complete spectrum of scents and flavours. It was a young, very attentive waiter who gave us this valuable advice.

With the cheese (Cantal, *bleu*, Saint-Thomas – about 60F) we tried a 1974 Moulin-à-Vent, just as sumptuous and mature, and perhaps even more full-bodied than the 1976 Fleurie. On a more recent visit, neither of these two wines was on offer any more but there was a 1983 Moulin-à-Vent for 150F a litre bottle. No telling which *millésime* (vintage year) will be on offer when my readers get there!

The Saint-Thomas cheese, by the way, has a fantasy name given to this farmhouse cheese by the Burgundian farmer who makes it. You can sample it at the *zinc* for 19F with bread, just like another Burgundy cheese, Rigotte, a cow's milk cheese from near Lyons in the form of small cylinders of about four centimetres in diameter and a little less in height.

Desserts are available at 24F: *tarte, gâteau, mousse au chocolat* . . .

With two cups of coffee, our bill came to about 700F for three, a lot of money, but a good 300F of it paid for a unique wine experience which, aside from yielding immense pleasure, was very interesting and instructive as well.

You can eat here abundantly for 150F to 160F including good wine, at just about any hour of the day until five in the morning. Countless are the times that I have had a good *andouillette* (chitterling sausage) grilled (53F) or cooked in white Pouilly-sur-Loire wine (58F) with crisp chips, preceded by a tomato salad (16F), followed by some cheese or a piece of cake and accompanied by a delicious half-bottle of Fleurie, around three o'clock in the morning. For *"Le Duc est à votre service jour et nuit"*. Bravo, Monsieur Georgé!

Open: *Until 5 am*
Closed: *Sunday*
Métro: *8, 9 Richelieu Drouot*   **Map:** *1*
Approximate price: *160F*

Chez Léon (Le Rubis)

10 rue du Marché-Saint-Honoré
Tel: 42.61.03.34

The place du Marché-Saint-Honoré is a pleasant, quiet square between the Tuileries gardens and the Opéra, with some shops, cafés, restaurants . . . all grouped around a large market hall converted into a fire station in the centre. A few steps away, on the corner of the rue du Marché-Saint-Honoré and the rue Saint-Hyacinthe is to be found one of the most bustling and authentic of Parisian wine bistros. From seven in the morning until ten in the evening you can taste, drink, sip, savour, just about everything that the Beaujolais region has to offer: simple and not so simple red wines by the glass, from an ordinary Beaujolais for 6F (prices per 8cl) via a sumptuous Côte-de-Brouilly (7.50F), to a full-bodied Fleurie or Moulin-à-Vent (8F).

The quality of the wines is excellent. The 1988 Fleurie, for instance, has a discreet aroma and is full of flavour and concentration, certainly not over-refined with too much sugar. A fact not to be under-estimated in an era when, for purely commercial reasons, much Beaujolais wine has been pepped up to a higher alcoholic content with a dose of sugar that flattens the flavour and deprives the wine of its character, bringing it down to the level of an insipid alcoholic lemonade which could (and often does) come from anywhere.

There is always a good white Mâcon-Clessé for 6F per 8cl, also recommended by the *patron:* a fresh, pure and authentic wine.

There are another twenty-five wines available by the glass. A few more examples: a Bourgeuil, a wonderfully fruity red Loire wine, costs 4.50F, a Cheverny from the Sauvignon grape (from a region south west of Orléans) is 4.50F too, while a surprisingly delicious white Côtes-du-Rhône is available for 4F and a delightfully mellow Coteaux-du-Layon for 4.50F. The Chinon (the left bank cousin of the Bourgeuil) costs 5.50F. And you can also have a bottle of Bordeaux or a Saint-Emilion served to you from a selection of about fifteen different years and growers, for between 45F and 350F (1985 Château La Lagune).

Every day at midday (until about three-thirty in the afternoon) one or two classic hot bistro dishes are served. Monday: *saucisson chaud* (hot pork sausage, a Lyons speciality – 35F), Tuesday: *tripes* or *tête de veau* (calf's head – 45F), Wednesday: *petit salé aux lentilles* (salt pork with lentils), or *plat-de-côtes* (stewed rib of beef – 45F), Thursday: *andouillette grillée pommes vapeur* (grilled chitterling sausage with steamed potatoes – 45F), Friday: *jarret aux lentilles* (shin of pork with lentils – 45F) or *boudin pommes vapeur* (black pudding with steamed potatoes – 35F). These dishes could serve as an introductory vacation course in *"savoir vivre"*. Tuition fee: 205F to 215F per person for five days. This basic diet could be supplemented each evening with a generous plate of assorted *charcuterie* or cheeses for 30F or 40F (according to size) or, in the summer months, with a salad of boiled beef (40F).

These tasty, wholesome and genuinely French meals, accompanied by one or two glasses of good wine, can be rounded off every once in a while by a sumptuous dessert: tarts with seasonal fruits or *tarte Tatin* (caramelised upside down apple tart) for 20F, *mousse au chocolat, crème caramel, clafoutis aux fruits* (batter open tart with fruit) for 18F, will not cost more than 700F for a five-day week, and the cheerful, lively, ever-changing company is entirely free. Don't ever under-estimate the "nutritional" value of atmosphere. During my recent visit to **Le Rubis** I made a note concerning wine appreciation: "The 'intrinsic' qualities of a wine reveal themselves only in the appropriate 'context' of food, ambiance, decor, noise, people . . . They simply do not exist in isolation and the *dégustateur-connoisseur* is nothing but an abstract chemical analysing machine imbibing wine and exhaling words". You are not really enjoying eating to its full capacity if you are busy counting calories and carbohydrates, and unable to appreciate freely the sensations transmitted by your tastebuds and the human warmth of the company.

From midday onwards, it is almost impossible to get one of the scant twenty-four seats at one of the few small tables on the ground floor, but there is also a dining room upstairs. If you come before twelve, however, you can find a table on the ground floor, where you can eat comfortably and have a quiet glass of wine (or two).

At the (real!) *zinc* slices of Poilâne bread (baked from naturally fermented sourdough) and other French (white) bread are available with *pâté de foie* (liver pâté) or *saucisson à l'ail* (air-dried garlic sausage) for 10F, excellent *rillettes* (minced pork slowly cooked in its own fat with spices and white wine) or rustic pork pâté, both for 14F, or cheese: Camembert, Saint-Nectaire, Gruyère, *chèvre*, for between 12 and 18F.

The *zinc* is almost always bustling like a beehive and the fact that there are three or four waitresses during peak hours may serve as an indication of the popularity of this old wine bistro. The atmosphere is informal, almost chummy. On warm, sunny days you can honour Bacchus on the pavement too, around a few large wine barrels.

Open: *6.45 am to 10 pm; Saturday: 9 am to 6 pm*
Closed: *Sunday*
Métro: *7 Pyramides; 1 Tuileries; 3,7,8 Opéra*   **Map:** *1*
Approximate price: *90F*
No reservations

Le Ruban Bleu
29 rue d'Argenteuil
Tel: 42.61.47.53

Just behind the stately avenue de l'Opéra between the rue des Pyramides and the rue Saint-Roch, in the rather quiet rue d'Argenteuil, you will find the small, cosy **Le Ruban Bleu**, named after the trophy won by the French ocean liner Normandie in June 1935 for the fastest crossing of the Atlantic ocean: in four days, three hours and two minutes. The food and drink-loving writer Colette was aboard.

After being escorted to a small table by the friendly *patronne*, and while sipping the house aperitif, a Montlouis *pétillant à la mûre sauvage* (slightly sparkling Loire wine with mild blackberry liqueur) I slowly absorb the décor and atmosphere of the small, well-lit dining room. A playfully undulating stuccoed blue ribbon frames a triptych of artfully cut mirrors on the long wall opposite the service counter. On upholstered benches and chairs there is room for about twenty-eight guests, and in a cosy niche in the back, another twelve people can be seated. It is rather crowded on the day of my visit to **Le Ruban Bleu** but there is not the slightest hint of haste or unrest disturbing the relaxed atmosphere. Lots of business people are enjoying themselves here, feasting with visible satisfaction on the delicacies provided by the fine kitchen and cellar.

The *cellier du mois* department of the bill of fare features three wines: a white and a red Menetou-Salon, grown, made and bottled by Henri Pellé at 95F and 52F a bottle and a half bottle respectively, a Saumur-Champigny 1988 from the Domaine des Galmoises of Pasquier Didier at Chacé at 96F and 52F, and a Cahors 1985, produced by the Comte de Monpezat and costing 96F a bottle. Entrées around 42F include a terrine, a *crottin chaud* (warm goat's cheese), a *salade de museau de boeuf* (ox muzzle salad), *frisée aux foies de volaille* (curly endive with chicken livers, a very popular French starter), a poached egg on an artichoke heart . . .

I opted for the *saumon cru mariné au citron* (raw salmon marinated in lemon juice), the most expensive entrée after the *foie gras de canard* (72F), and very tender and tasty – something that I will not forget easily. This delicacy was followed by an irreproachable *steak de gigot d'agneau* (slice of leg of lamb) with fresh noodles, something not often found in a Paris restaurant (90F). Two regular customers from Rouen who noticed the fresh pasta on my plate from their table, asked the *patronne* a little disapprovingly why she had not advised them that there was fresh pasta that day.

Other dishes on the menu: *confit de canard* – 95F, *haddock à la Curnonsky* (smoked haddock, poached and served on a bed of spinach with a poached egg on top and melted butter) – 92F. A portion of remarkably delicious Brie de Meaux (32F) and a gigantic piece of *tarte fine aux pommes et son sorbet de Calvados* (light apple tart with Calvados sorbet) for 35F gave the final touch to this memorable meal which I had accompanied by the cool Saumur-Champigny. It was only the disappointingly high price (around 45F as it is everywhere) that kept me from having an *eau-de-vie* with my coffee (12F).

I specially appreciated: the house aperitif, the irreproachable and wholesome quality of the dishes, the extremely attentive and efficient service. You are almost unaware that it's there, and that is the way it should be.

It is perhaps worth mentioning that this bistro has been honoured by the Syndicate of Parisian *chefs de cuisine* with the Curnonsky medal which is mounted on the wall above a bench and which reads: *"Cette place était celle de Maurice Edmond Saillant dit Curnonsky – Prince élu des Gastronomes – Hôte d'honneur de cette maison"* – "This was the habitual seat of Maurice Edmond Saillant (1872–1956), alias Curnonsky, elected Prince of Gastronomes (in 1927) and honoured guest of this house". The dish of smoked haddock mentioned above was also named after this eminent epicure who always praised simplicity and authenticity, principles that are indeed followed by **Le Ruban Bleu**.

Closed: *Every night and Sunday all day*
Métro: *7 Pyramides*   **Map:** *1*
Approximate price: *270F*

Runtz
16 rue Favart
Tel: 42.96.69.86

It is tempting to find a redecorated restaurant more attractive than the old original, even more so when exposed to the owners' gleefully expressed pride. In the case of **Runtz** (formerly **Au Gourmet d'Alsace**) it took a while for my feelings of nostalgia for the original décor, burnished with use, to be followed by real appreciation of the newly furnished and decorated, well-lit and enlarged dining room.

The entrance from the rue d'Amboise gives access to the bar while the one around the corner, on the rue Favart, leads directly into the dining area.

The red Pinot Noir d'Alsace that I had savoured at the wood-covered *zinc* in the spring of 1985 is still from the same good grower, Gustave Lorentz at Bergheim, although now, five years later, it is no longer a 1982 but a 1987, and today it costs 12F instead of 10F, which is a very modest increase indeed. Oh yes, and it is called "Rosé d'Alsace" now (because it comes in litre bottles and therefore may not be sold under any other name).

The cheerful *patronne*, Madame Odette Leport, is still the same too (although she frequently changes her glasses and her hairdo so that it is sometimes difficult to recognise her) and it is her maiden name that serves as the new name because, she explained, there are already far too many restaurants and *brasseries* in Paris called "Alsace" in one way or another. The Leport family wanted to distinguish themselves by their choice of name, as they have already done by the quality of their food and wine; a fact that inspired me to write in the first edition of my guide in 1985: "How many among the hungry crowds on the nearby boulevard des Italiens would like to find a little place like this and save themselves the disappointment of an over-expensive and frequently inferior tourist trap along the *grands boulevards!*"

My old enthusiasm was re-kindled when I sat on a comfortable chair at one of the small tables ranged along the wall. The chairs are covered with a dark red velvet that makes you think of the cinema or of the neighbouring Opéra Comique (Salle Favart entrance: place Boieldieu; Favart and Boieldieu were seventeenth and eighteenth century French composers, and it may be of interest that it was the Parisian Charles Simon Favart, originally a pastry cook, who first created musical comedy).

Preskopf, jellied head of pork with potato and green salad (38F), is my entrée, while my companion chooses *salade strasbourgeoise,* coarsely-grated Gruyère, slices of *cervelat* sausage and hard-boiled egg on a bed of green salad, for the same price.

As main dishes, two traditional specialities of the old **Gourmet d'Alsace** are brought to the table. A *choucroute de poissons* (sauerkraut with fish) for 84F, and a *jambonneau grillé,* grilled hock of pork for 64F. Poached, the same *jambonneau* is on the menu with the epithet *"comme à Strasbourg"* and costs 61F.

The sauerkraut and fish dish that I remembered from a previous visit consists of fillets of poached smoked haddock and monkfish on a bed of creamy, not-too-sour sauerkraut accompanied by thin slices of bacon, and mussels. The chef's style (the *patronne's* husband) is clearly expressed in this dish, and my companion, who is experiencing this combination for the first time, as I had done a few years earlier, is visibly enjoying it.

My hock of pork, which turns out to be a gargantuan quantity of meat on the bone, is delicious and almost enough for two. The accompanying potatoes are a marvel of consistency and flavour. The white Alsatian Riesling is fresh and aromatic, priced at 43F a half-litre carafe (21.50F for 25cl). I skipped the cheese, Munster de la Vallée with caraway seed (27F) that I had enjoyed so much on a previous occasion, for sheer lack of space after the *jambonneau*, and in order to accommodate a *fôret-noir* (32F) (Black Forest gâteau). A chef's masterpiece! My friend had to content himself with a piece of fresh cheesecake for 28F, because the *fôret-noir* had sold out (make sure to order your helping at the beginning of the meal). He was soon consoled by the cheesecake: every product from Monsieur Leport's oven is a special treat.

The coffee is good and costs 13F for a small cup accompanied by chocolates and small, crisp meringues.

At the end of the meal, I devoted a few minutes to scrutinising the bill of fare once more. As well as the sauerkraut, either with mixed fish or with monkfish (80F), there are four others with ham (*jambonneau*), with sausage and bacon, and with all three (*choucroute Gourmet*) for 60F, 62F and 98F respectively, while the black pudding (*boudin noir*) with fried apple and sauerkraut is available for 64F.

Two fish dishes (smoked haddock 79F, and salmon 83F) and three meat dishes (beef 102F, lamb 73F, veal 88F) complete the list of **Runtz**'s wholesome, well-prepared and generously served fare.

There are ten entrées with a *tarte à l'oignon chaude* (warm onion tart – 29F) and home-made *foie gras de canard* (69F) among them.

Among the special suggestions, I discovered a very extraordinary dish, not easily found on any restaurant bill of fare but served here each Thursday: *bäeckeoffa*, literally, baker's oven, a traditional example of Alsatian family cooking. Mutton shoulder, loin of pork, and beef, marinated and baked for hours in white wine, together with onions, carrots and potatoes. Not sauerkraut but *backeofe* (the spelling is variable) is real Alsatian country cooking. Traditionally, Monday was wash-day in Alsace. Housewives who did not have time to prepare a midday meal, solved the problem by sending their earthenware dishes with the meat in its marinade, sliced potatoes, onions and carrots arranged in layers, to the local bakery where they were all put in the baker's oven for a few hours. At noon, one of the children was sent to fetch the *bäckeoffe* from the bakery.

I caught up on the opportunity to try this exceptional regional speciality at **Runtz**'s the following Thursday. Cool crisp Riesling in pretty Alsatian wine glasses (long green stem, small round bowls), heated plates, glowing hot earthenware pans with steaming broth and all the pleasure I had imagined from the description given above!

76F is the price of this culinary adventure, and I now sampled my beloved Munster cheese too, accompanied by a small carafe of fragrant spicy Gewürztraminer (25.50F) while my companion tasted a *tarte vosgienne*, a raspberry tart from the Vosges mountains, intimately related to the *fôret-noir*.

On Thursdays booking is imperative – when we arrived the place was filled to capacity.

You can have a late supper here, too, by the way (*Opéra Comique oblige*). Orders are taken until midnight.

Open: *10 am to 12 pm*
Closed: *Saturday and Sunday*
Métro: *3 Quatre-Septembre; 8,9 Richelieu Drouot* **Map:** *1*
Approximate price: *195F*

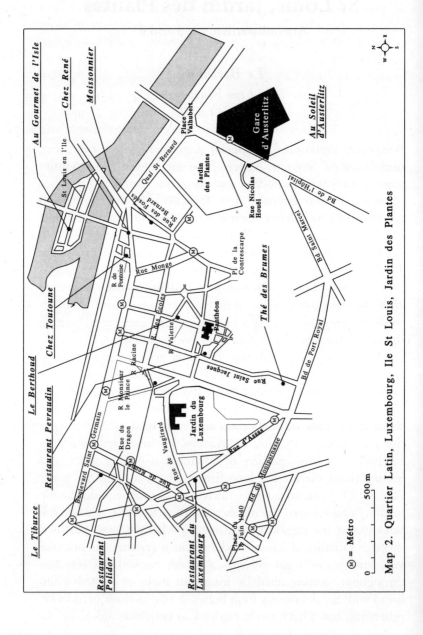

Map 2. Quartier Latin, Luxembourg, Ile St Louis, Jardin des Plantes

Ⓜ = Métro

0   500 m

Quartier Latin, Luxembourg, Ile St Louis, Jardin des Plantes

Arrondissements 4, 5 and 6

Le Berthoud
1 rue Valette
Tel: 43.54.38.81

A special restaurant, a special *patronne-chef de cuisine*, the multi-talented Suzanne Knych. The menu, three typewritten pages, firmly and explicitly sets down the laudable principles observed in the kitchen: it is formally guaranteed that no commercial concentrates (meat glaze or stock) or artificial flavours will be used and that none of the meat has been frozen.

The vegetables are always fresh, even those of the *gratiné Vivaldi*, an oven-browned dish of vegetables from every season (80F or 85F with poached eggs or a Toulouse sausage simmered with the *gratin*), one of five different *gratins* on the list. Another speciality is egg dishes, eight in total for 65F each, not counting the *oeufs coque pain grillé et notre beurre personnel* (35F).

Let me begin by explaining the *beurre personnel*: it is prepared each day from fresh cream without any colouring, flavouring or preservative and it is *delicious*! Now, about the eggs: the white and the yolk are both cooked to the same degree of fluidity, with the white thoroughly white, but still uniformly fluid, a result that, to my knowledge, can only be reached by immersing the eggs carefully in a large quantity of hot but not boiling water, and leaving them there for a long time without heating the water further. This can take up to thirty minutes, depending on the quantity of the water, the number and the size of the eggs and the thickness of the eggshells. Madame Knych must have her own speedier variation of this method, because it certainly did not take very long before I got my eggs, perfectly cooked and very hot throughout, accompanied by long thin sticks of toasted white bread with the deliciously fresh butter. It may perhaps sound a bit ridiculous, but I have rarely enjoyed an entrée so much, lost in silent admiration for the perfection of each constituent part and for the harmony of the whole: a simple and honest work of art!

The *hachis Parmentier* (80F) which I chose as a main course is a baked dish composed of a layer of finely chopped boiled beef between two layers of mashed potatoes, a time-honoured recipe for using left-over meat, similar to an English shepherd's pie. This simple dish, very attractively described by Balzac in *Le Cousin Pons*, has been in vogue in Paris for a few years now but the **Le Berthoud** version is much more authentic than one I tried a few days earlier at the counter of a rather fashionable wine bar.

At **Le Berthoud** I accompanied the *hachis* with a green salad seasoned with lemon juice and olive oil from Ampus in Provence, one of nine salads on the menu for between 35 and 50F.

Other main-course options from the menu: *quenelles de brochet* (poached dumplings of pike), *gratinées*, or in a light lemon sauce or in a spinach or pepper sauce, for 70F, *canard aux olives* (duck) – 95F, *côte de veau* (veal chop) – 95F, grilled beef or lamb – 95F without, and 100F with a sauce.

I tried the red 1982 Clos Toumilon from the Graves region, south of Bordeaux for 90F (50F for a half bottle), but found it less convincing than the young, fresh, aromatic Gamay de Touraine at 55F produced by wine grower Henry Marionnet at Soings-en-Sologne that I drank with a magnificent *pot-au-feu* (boiled beef with vegetables – 95F) a few days before.

Le Berthoud is famous for its *pot-au-feu* and you should try it here if you have never had it before (and certainly if you've had it and liked it, too). On an oval plate garnished with a large carrot, two leeks, two turnips, a large boiled potato and two marrow bones, there was a generous piece of excellent meat, accompanied by coarse salt in a small brown earthenware vessel. It is not only good, copious and authentic, but also stylish and unpretentious.

That goes for the décor of this split-level restaurant, too: old-fashioned lamps with porcelain shades; large film posters (*Les Enfants du Paradis*) and huge modern paintings by Suzanne Knych on the walls; lace curtains and tiled mosaic floors. The clientèle here seems rather serious: about their conversation or about what they are eating or both. But the atmosphere is neither sombre nor hectic. As it is always crowded here in the evenings (orders are accepted until one o'clock in the morning!) you should definitely reserve your table well in advance. But at lunch you can have an extended meal in peace and sample some of the numerous specialities of this excellent restaurant. It is not mentioned in any of the guides I know, although it has been here for almost 25 years just a few steps from the Panthéon, at the corner of the rue de l'Ecole Polytechnique.

But the culinary talents of Suzanne Knych have not gone unnoticed: she was made *commandeur des cordon bleus de France* at Dijon on the 4th of November 1989. An especially proficient and skilful female chef is called a *cordon bleu* in France. And Madame Knych proudly wears the insignia of her rank on her white cook's uniform while she moves from table to table, ensuring that everything has been to each client's satisfaction.

That was certainly the case after I had finished my *pot-au-feu.* I was then ready to order some cheese or a dessert from the two-page list of desserts, teas (Ceylon, China, Russia, blackberry, limeflower, mint, verbena . . . – 20F), coffee (20F), *digestives* (50F, 60F, and 75F), and champagnes (200F and 360F a bottle, 70F a quarter of a bottle and 110F half a bottle). Cheeses cost 50F (Camembert, *chèvre* (goat), or home-made fresh soft cheese with cream or honey), and there are fourteen different desserts all at the same price, mostly on a puff-pastry base *(feuilletage)*, and with curious names like *volupté, damnation,* and *bellissimo.*

I took the *fruits à l'eau-de-vie blanche faits par nous* (fruit in aromatic liqueur distilled from ripe fruit) which turned out to be sweet and potent.

Coffee (20F) is served here as a good espresso on an octagonal black tray with a crystal glass of cold water, a small glass plate with brown and white sugar cubes, and some soft chocolate with almond shavings wrapped in aluminium foil. A worthy finale to a delightful, stylish meal; one prepared by a cook who not only loves and masters her *métier,* but is also a painter and a philosopher.

Open: *Until 1 am*
Closed: *Saturday at midday and Sunday all day*
Métro: *10 Maubert-Mutualité*   **Map:** *2*
Approximate price: *240F*

Restaurant du Luxembourg
44 rue d'Assas
Tel: 45.48.90.22

Readers of this guidebook will perhaps arrive at this traditionally-furnished little restaurant coming from the Jardin du Luxembourg. After passing the tennis courts, you cross the rue Guynemer and then the rue Madame and after a few steps along the rue Fleurus, you are walking straight towards the browny-red façade of the **Restaurant du Luxembourg** on the corner of the rue d'Assas. Most of the regulars, however, come from offices in the vicinity at midday while a few elderly people living in the neighbourhood also take their meals here frequently.

The restaurant changed ownership in 1984, and the new young *patron*, after some initial difficulties, managed to maintain and even enlarge its regular *clientèle*. But while the décor, fortunately, has not changed, the character of the *cuisine* has been streamlined a bit. Dishes such as calf's brains and sheep's kidneys have been replaced by *bavette grillée pommes Pont-Neuf* (grilled skirt of beef with French fried potatoes – 40F) and *confit de canard pommes sautées* (preserved duck with sautéed potatoes – 76F).

The bill of fare is no longer handwritten every day, but there is still a daily special dish for 38F. Examples: *carré de porc, purée mousseline* (rack of pork with mashed potatoes), *jambon au porto épinards* (braised ham in port with spinach) . . .

I had two deliciously tender lamb chops (which I prefer lightly underdone, *rosé* – and they were perfectly cooked to order) with crisp *pommes Pont-Neuf*, named after Paris' oldest bridge, dating from the reign of Henri IV, where French fried potatoes were sold until the end of the last century at little market stalls along the parapet for five *centimes* without salt. Salt was another five *centimes*.

At an adjacent table, a gentleman was eating a *filet de haddock* with *pommes à l'anglaise* (poached smoked haddock with boiled potatoes – 55F) with visible gusto.

As entrée I had an excellently prepared tomato salad (15F), far superior to the careless heap of flabby tomato slices with a tired *vinaigrette* which is too often served, and not just in the less expensive establishments.

Other entrées on the bill of fare: *émincé de champignons frais* (fresh sliced, seasoned mushrooms – 20F), *oeuf en gelée* (egg in jelly – 20F), or a hard-boiled egg with mayonnaise and shredded carrots – 22F.

At midday, the most expensive dish on offer is the *filet de boeuf au poivre* (fillet of beef with pepper – 86F) while the bill of fare at dinner lists the *bavette* at 48F as the cheapest dish and additionally offers a *filet de saumon à l'oseille* (salmon with sorrel) for 76F.

Desserts cost between about 15F (fruit, *crème caramel*) and 35F (*tarte Tatin* – caramelised apple tart). The fruit tart (22F) is copious but not exceptional.

I took a small wedge of Camembert (14F). There is also Gruyère for the same price, while Pont-l'Evêque and Roquefort cost 19F each. *Chèvre* (goat's cheese) is available at 16F.

The house wines on offer per 25cl carafe (11F, 12F, and 23F) are all *négociant*-bottled, so I am not recommending any of them, but there is quite an extensive list of *château*-bottled red Bordeaux from the 1982 vintage onward for prices between 76F (a 1986 Côtes-de-Bourg) and 320F (1982 Château Croizet-Bages). For the more modest drinkers, and more in keeping with the simple *cuisine*, there is a 1985 Cahors from a good producer (Georges Vigouroux) at 85F, also available in half-bottles (47F).

The **Luxembourg** is rather crowded at midday, but the atmosphere never becomes hectic. The service, by a hardworking waiter with black hair, a black moustache, a black waistcoat and trousers, and white shirt with black bow tie, is prompt and correct.

The welcome by the young patron, Monsieur Pommereau, is very friendly and he will help guests into their overcoats when they leave. People of all ages settle easily into the warm and convivial atmosphere of the **Restaurant du Luxembourg**. And you can get a decent three-course meal with a bottle of beer (8F) and coffee for as little as 85F.

I specially appreciated: the tomato salad, the *plat du jour*, and the atmosphere which encourages contact between the generations.

Open: *12 to 2.30 pm and 7.15 pm to 9.30 pm*
Closed: *Saturday night and Sunday all day*
Métro: *4 Saint-Placide, or 12 Notre-Dame-des-Champs* **Map:** *2*
Approximate price: *120F*

Moissonnier
28 rue des Fossés-Saint-Bernard
Tel: 43.29.87.65

Just the place to eat well, copiously and in good company on a Sunday afternoon after a visit to the Musée d'Orsay, I thought, when I decided to book a table at this solid restaurant specialising in dishes from the Lyons region and the adjoining Franche Comté. Luckily, there was still a small table available when I telephoned at eleven – good eating places charging reasonable prices and open on Sundays are not easily found in Paris and the demand is great.

Coming from the Seine and walking up the rue des Fossés-Saint-Bernard, I could spot above a red canopy the narrow black sign with nothing but the word **Moissonnier** inscribed in gold letters. The present owner's father had been *patron* of **La Chope Danton** on the boulevard Saint-Germain. But the increasingly oppressive tourist rush there finally prompted the Moissonniers to abandon that spot and to settle down in a quieter neighbourhood where their kitchen and wine cellar, unconditionally committed to high-quality products and cherished by their faithful clientèle, could be maintained at their level of excellence.

The *saladiers lyonnais* (50F per person) underline this just as much as the *breuzi de Franche Comté* (alternatively spelt *brési*, cured smoked and air-dried fillet of beef served in wafer-thin slices – 45F), the *rosette de Lyon* (air-dried, sliced pork sausage – 40F), the *quenelles de brochet* (dumplings of pike mousse – 80F), the *tablier de sapeur sauce gribiche* (fried bread-crumbed tripe in the shape of what used to be a fireman's apron – 85F), or the *gras double sauté Lyonnais* (stew of the best parts of ox tripe – 85F). The *plateau des fromages jurassiens et cervelle de canut* (literally, silk weaver's brain – Lyons used to have a large silk industry; a home-made blend of fermented curds, shallots, chervil and other herbs, white wine, *crème fraîche* and, optionally, olive oil) costs 35F and desserts (eleven in total, all of them home-made) are available at between 30F and 40F. Regional and house specialities are handwritten with red ink on the menu, while more common dishes, such as *carré d'agneau, contrefilet grillé* and others, are marked in black ink.

Current wines are served in *pots* here. A *pot* is a heavy bottle of thick, colourless glass with a capacity of 46cl, formerly customary in the Beaujolais region. The wine in this stable container stays cool for a longer time.

White wines are from the area around Mâcon (Mâcon-Villages 1987) and the Arbois region (1987), priced at 60F and 65F respectively for 46cl. Four red wines, one from Saint-Nicolas-de-Bourgueil in the Loire valley (1987 – 45F), two growths from the Beaujolais – a 1989 Côte-de-Brouilly and 1989 Morgon at 65F each – and a 1987 Arbois for the same price, complete the list of *pots*.

Naturally, there is a more extensive list of red and white vintage Burgundies and Bordeaux wines back to 1981, for prices between 130F and 520F a bottle. There are also some very rare Jura wines such as Vin Jaune 1978 at 280F and Château Chalon 1979 at 380F. These wines have matured for at least six years in wooden casks and their taste is reminiscent of sherry. They come in 62cl bottles (to compensate for the amount of wine evaporated during the long maturing period).

I started with a generous glass of the white Arbois (30F), served by the friendly *patronne* at my table near the service counter, a solid wooden affair with carvings of bunches of grapes. The wine was fresh, scented and full of flavour, with a hint of sherry in the taste. A perfect aperitif. The *kir* (white wine with a little blackcurrant liqueur – 15F) is poured ready-mixed from a litre bottle kept behind the counter.

My entrée was the *saucisson chaud* (45F): six thick slices of lightly pink pork sausage with six potatoes attractively cut in even shapes. The sausage was firm, not fatty but somewhat lacking in taste. The Côte-de-Brouilly (65F) that I drank with it was light in colour and scent, and pure in flavour.

In the meantime, the dining room filled up and some new arrivals were shown upstairs to the first-floor dining room with its vaulted ceiling and Beaujolais barrels protruding from brick walls. On the ground floor the dining room is divided by a huge bench. Since I faced the entrance I could see the expressions on the faces of newcomers: unpretentious, hopeful, optimistic . . . most of them are obviously old friends and welcomed with handshakes.

At an adjoining table the *saladiers lyonnais* were being served . . . twelve large earthenware salad bowls containing red cabbage, lentils, brown and green beans, sausages, pork brawn, boiled beef, marinated herring fillets . . . Everyone helps himself to whatever he likes with a wooden fork and spoon. A convivial and festive way to start a meal and a real bargain at a mere 50F a head, which I had tried on a previous visit.

At the table next to mine, an elderly couple who have been eating here regularly for years and years have ordered a plate of *pétoncles farcis* (85F): flat queen scallops stuffed with seasoned herb butter and browned in the oven. They share one dish, an option reserved for regulars.

At my own table, two large pike dumplings, *quenelles de brochet*, in a light smooth tomato sauce, are set down before me. The *quenelles* are really extraordinarily large and I quite understand my neighbour, who has ordered the same dish and is eating only one of them.

Time for some cheese now, and a second *pot* of Côte-de-Brouilly; the *patronne* tells me that I only have to pay for what I drink. From a large bowl, Madame Moissonnier ladles out portions of *cervelle de canut* which she has prepared with chives and lots of *crème fraîche*. The selection of cheeses from the Jura accompanying this includes Tête de Moine scraped from a four-inch thick cylinder with a special device yielding small bits looking rather like cauliflower florets and soft, pungent Vacherin, with a reddish rind in a chip box. The Côte-de-Brouilly is excellent with these cheeses.

Classic bistro desserts on the bill of fare such as *mousse au chocolat aux zestes d'orange, gâteau de riz, gâteau au chocolat amer sauce pistache* are complemented by two or three ice creams and sorbets. The *oeufs à la neige* are two gigantic puffs of soft meringue garnished with almond slivers, floating on a vanilla custard – it seems as if all dishes here are double portions. At another table, a *sorbet aux framboises sauvages* is being savoured together with a glass of pink Arbois wine by a solitary gentleman.

Around a quarter to three, I hear the word *"café"* for the first time and the *patron*, Monsieur Moissonnier, clad in a white chef's vest, who has come down from the first floor where he had been dividing his attention between the kitchen and the dining room, pours coffee (10F) from a large glass Cona jug into the cups that have been set down at tables. The freshly prepared coffee tastes good in this homely atmosphere.

"A genuine Sunday lunch which leaves nothing to be desired," I said to myself when leaving **Moissonnier**'s dining room in a very good mood and completely content.

Of course, you can dine here on weekdays (except Monday) too: noon and night.

Open: *12 to 2.30 pm and 7 to 10 pm*
Closed: *Sunday night and Monday all day. August*
Métro: *10 Cardinal-Lemoine or 7, 10 Jussien*   **Map:** *2*
Approximate price: *245F*

Restaurant Perraudin
157 rue Saint-Jacques
Tel: 46.33.15.75

This is one of those places you can walk past hundreds of times. The old-fashioned sobriety which marks or rather conceals the front of this old restaurant is confirmed by the impression created by the spacious dining room inside.

The carefully handwritten menu displayed in a front window invites the interested reader by offering a choice of classic dishes: thirteen entrées for between 16F and 24F, seven main courses for 45F, 48F and 58F, four carefully selected cheeses at 10F (Camembert de Normandie) and 12F (raw goat's cheese, Brie de Meaux, farmhouse Reblochon) and some desserts for around 20F.

However, the main attraction of this quiet establishment is the daily *menu spécial midi* for 59F served at midday only and offering a choice of three entrées:*champignons à la grecque* (marinated button mushrooms), hot *pâté en croûte* and a tart of fresh cream cheese and ham. Three main dishes include sauerkraut with three different *charcuteries*, casseroled rabbit *(civet de lapin)*, and farmhouse chicken with onions. The main dishes change each day. To finish, cheese or a simple dessert are available.

Carefully prepared family cooking has been the stock-in-trade of this bistro for decades, and still is, although the dining room, formerly divided in two by a glass partition, has now gained in atmosphere by being more spaciously fitted, with large mirrors on the walls and lots of space between the simple tables and chairs.

I had my most recent meal at **Restaurant Perraudin** at a small table between the front windows and the old buffet, covered with the customary red and white check cloth and furnished with a large earthenware pitcher of water. You are served by young waitresses who are not always beaming with cheerfulness. But then it would be just as mistaken to take this personally, as it is to think that a stereotyped waiter's smile is meant to express a special affection for you – although it is tempting to entertain that idea.

My entrée was *gnocchi à la parisienne*, oven-browned dumplings of mashed potatoes garnished with tomato and parsley, after a 12F glass of cool, refreshingly acidulous Pineau de Touraine from the grower Jean-Marie Penet (Pineau is the local name for the white Chenin grape, indigenous in the Loire valley). *Kir* is 8F and obviously made with a less expensive white wine, the sweetness of the blackcurrant liqueur amply camouflaging any possibly disagreeable or unsatisfactory flavour . . . as is true with *kir* anywhere nine times out of ten.

The *rôti de porc aux pruneaux* (roast pork with prunes), served with a generous helping of oven-browned cauliflower, is good without leaving a lasting impression – which perhaps would be expecting too much from such a simple and inexpensive dish.

My red wine is the 1988 Saint-Nicolas-de-Bourgueil from the grower Joël Bureau at "La Forcine" and proves a very fitting companion for this simple, wholesome meal. It is reasonably priced at 68F (40F for a half bottle).

The clientèle is composed of parties of two and three with a comparatively large proportion of solitary eaters – as has, oddly enough, always been the case here ever since my first visit about six years ago, in spite of the changed ownership and décor.

I chose a *bavarois framboise* (26F) (raspberry Bavarian cream) as my dessert after a selection of three cheeses for 24F. Coffee is available at 8F a cup but I opted for a *café filtre à l'ancienne* with an individual metal filtering device on top of a dark green earthenware cup. This is only 9F and is served with a small cigar-shaped piece of chocolate.

One of the special features of **Restaurant Perraudin** is that there are always two or three good wines available by the glass for 12F to 15F. The fixed-price three-course menu is well composed and always good value for money, and the décor and the atmosphere are genuine and comfortably old-fashioned.

Closed: Saturday and Sunday
Métro: RER B Luxembourg   *Map:* 2
Approximate price: 145F
Fixed-price menu: 59F (midday)

Restaurant Polidor
41 rue Monsieur-le-Prince
Tel: 43.26.95.34

This is a well-known address, familiar for decades to countless Parisians and visitors, situated near the famous Odéon Theatre: **Crèmerie Restaurant Polidor**. Originally the bill of fare announced "carefully prepared meals", and a "recommended wine cellar"; in 1930 this was upgraded to "very carefully prepared meals".

Until about five years ago, the bill of fare promised *cuisine familiale* and nowadays, though nothing has really changed, neither the décor nor the cooking, the repertoire has been streamlined and offers two different specialities each day for between 40F and 60F, plus a series of five 56F two-course set menus served Monday to Friday at midday. While these items are still indicated in French alone, the fourteen regular entrées (including soup) (12F to 22F, 48F for a dozen snails) and the fifteen regular main dishes (40F to 60F) on the bill of fare are listed both in French and English. Original examples: *canard de Barbarie aux petits poix* – duck, 56F, *boeuf bourguignon* – 40F, *saucisson de Lyon pommes anglaises* – sausage, 46F, and so on. The *plats du jour*, however, because they are not on offer every day, can safely be assumed to be freshly prepared. And there are some interesting ones among them, such as tongue (*langue de boeuf*), served hot in a spicy sauce on Mondays (56F), *andouillette du Père Duval* (a chitterling sausage from one of Paris' best *charcutiers*) on Saturdays (60F), *darne de saumon au beurre blanc* (salmon fillet with a sauce of shallots, white wine, vinegar and lots of good butter) on Sundays (60F), or calf's sweetbread (*ris de veau à la crème*) on the same day and for the same price.

Large mirrors and old posters decorate the walls, with a few green plants here and there, a Thonet coat-stand in a corner, a stately buffet with one of those brass-framed *étagères* and a spiral staircase. A large oblong table for fourteen people occupies the centre of the dining room, surrounded by about six or seven tables for six. The place is regularly filled to capacity in the evenings and a lively hum of voices pervades the dining area where young waitresses quickly and efficiently bring plates, bottles and bowls to the paper-covered tables. There are a number of local regulars (a pigeonhole rack holds their cotton napkins – a fact that is invitingly indicated on the bill of fare), a few students and lots of tourists who frequently crowd the entrance (especially in the evenings) waiting for a place or a table either here or in a dining room in the back, seating about thirty people.

In this atmosphere bustling with activity and saturated with whiffs and puffs of intermingling conversations in various languages, seated at a table occupied by three ladies unknown to me, I tried the *champignons à la grecque* (14F) (a bit overspiced); and the *museau vinaigrette* (pork brawn – 14F) which I had enjoyed on an earlier visit. The *blanquette de veau citronée au riz* (56F) turned out to be a well-flavoured version of this eternal bistro classic: chunks of veal with button mushrooms in a creamy white sauce, flavoured with lemon juice and served with rice. It was aptly accompanied by **Polidor**'s house wine, a remarkable light red AOC Fronsac 1987 Château Magondeau (André Goujon, grower at Saillaus) which costs only 60F a bottle, or 30F a carafe of 33cl and 10F a glass. Other possibilities: *vin de pays* (32/16/6F), Cahors (48/24/18F) and some other wines for comparable prices. At lunch you could make do with a carafe of simple *vin rouge* at 7F for 25cl or a carafe of white Sauvignon for 21F (33cl).

The *tarte Tatin* (caramelised apple pie – 22F) which is on offer besides *baba au rhum* (rum cake – 14F), *gâteau de riz* (rice mould –

12F) and another six classic bistro desserts, is served in a generous portion. Including a cup of coffee (7F), my bill came to 129F, hardly more than I paid three years ago for about the same fare. Quite an accomplishment for a popular Paris restaurant in a notoriously inflationary era.

With an egg mayonnaise (12F), a traditional pork casserole (40F), followed by *mousse au chocolat* (12F), two glasses of Fronsac (20F) and a cup of coffee, you can even have an authentic French meal here for appreciably less than 100F without taking recourse to the amputated two-course set menu.

Notwithstanding its popularity and its low prices, **Polidor** has managed to keep up a good standard of traditional French *cuisine* and offers good wine at attractive prices. The words of the new owner who took over the establishment from Marie-Christine Kervela (now at **Perraudin**, rue Saint-Jacques, page 00) in 1987 were *"rien n'a changé"* (nothing has changed) and they have proved to be correct.

Polidor now has an offspring, launched about a year ago next door, at number 39, and called **Pol'nor** (Tel: 43.25.16.55), a rather chic ice-cream parlour with a cocktail bar attached. They make good sorbets and ice-creams (price about 30F); they have a set menu for 75F of smoked salmon, ice cream or sorbet, a glass of white wine, and a cup of coffee; and they serve American cocktails including Dry Martini, Manhattan and Bloody Mary for 35F until two in the morning. This is not exactly what you would call typically French, but it is good and **Pol'nor** might be a convenient place to wait until a table is available next door.

Open: *Seven days a week from 12 to 2.30 pm and 7 pm to 1 am (7 pm to 11 pm on Sunday)*
Métro: *4, 10 Odéon*   **Map:** *2*
Approximate price: *140F*

Au Soleil d'Austerlitz
18 boulevard de l'Hôpital
Tel: 43.31.22.38

This wine café (it doesn't quite seem a bistro) is located across from the left bank station, gare d'Austerlitz, just a few steps from the beautiful Jardin des Plantes, a large fenced green space comprising lawns with paths, benches and flower beds, lots of old trees and children's playgrounds, a very interesting botanical garden with a huge greenhouse, and a zoo.

On first sight, the **Soleil d'Austerlitz** looks like the kind of *brasserie* you can find near all the Paris stations, but this one is exceptionally well run and there is a fine selection of Beaujolais and Loire wines (plus a few others) per glass on offer which you can sample at the gleaming, brass-covered *zinc* in small quantities of 8cl (if you ask for *"un petit verre s'il vous plaît"*) or at a table in glasses containing 14cl. Prices for 14cl range from 18F for an interesting red Anjou-Villages (a recent *appellation* for ripened Cabernet Franc wine with a little Cabernet Sauvignon now and then from choice territories in the Anjou region), a good Chinon (pure Cabernet Franc, somewhat lighter), or a *kir* made in the authentic fashion with white Aligoté wine and blackcurrant liqueur, both from Burgundy; more ambitiously you can pay 25F for a prestigious Sancerre from the grower Denizot at Verdigny, or a rare and very agreeable 1988 Beaujolais *blanc* from the Cave des Vignerons de Lièrgues. Five Beaujolais *crus* (Côte-de-Brouilly, Morgon, Regnié, Juliénas, and Chénas) were available when I last visited at 23F a 14cl glass. 19F buys a glass of good Sauvignon de Touraine, one of Beaujolais *rosé* (very rare) or one of good Beaujolais-Villages. It is definitely more advantageous, however, to buy a 25cl pitcher at the table because the prices are 27F, 30F, and 35F respectively which amounts to a saving of more than ten per cent.

While all the wines come directly from the growers as befits a genuine wine bistro (André Calvet, the *patron* earned the *Meilleur Pot* award for the best wine *bistrotier* of the year in 1984), the list unfortunately does not give the growers' names, nor the wines' vintage years. The ones I tasted were all of recent vintages. But then André Calvet is a very amiable *patron* who learned his trade from another *bistrotier* and wine merchant who earned the *Meilleur Pot* award as long ago as in 1967 and who is also one of his suppliers. André Calvet calls him *"mon professeur"*.

Speaking about *"pots"*, the traditional 46cl Beaujolais bottle, you can also have a *pot* of red Coteaux-du-Lyonnais at 55F, the cheapest wine on the list. The charm of one of those heavy-based, thick bottles that were once popular in the Lyons region may add to the pleasure.

There is a hot *plat du jour* every day for around 60F. Examples: *filet de porc moutarde* (pork with mustard sauce), calf's liver, monkfish . . . You can start with a tomato salad for 20F and finish with a *tarte* or a *mousse au chocolat* for 27F. Together with a quarter of a litre of wine and a cup of coffee such a meal should not set you back more than 150F.

But there are also four different *mâchons* composed of local products (*charcuterie*, cheeses) from various provinces. (*Mâchon* is the Lyon expression for a hearty bite to eat with a glass of local wine.) The *mâchons* at the **Soleil d'Austerlitz** are all served with butter and Poilâne sourdough bread for 65F. An example: the *mâchon de l'Aveyron:* country ham, small frizzled cubes of duck *(fritons de canard)*, wild boar terrine, country sausage. For the same price you can have *la ronde de nos provinces*, a platter of five different cheeses served with nut-filled Poilâne bread. Or the perennial hot *saucisson de Lyon* with warm potato salad.

Choice enough in this lively wine café where you are easily enveloped in the warm, informal atmosphere. The service by waiters in long black aprons, white shirts and black ties is efficient and obliging.

On a March morning around eleven the whole **Soleil d'Austerlitz** on the corner of the rue Nicolas-Houël was bathed in bright sunshine coming from the direction of the gare d'Austerlitz as if to emphasise its name . . . .

Open: *6 am to 8 pm*
Closed: *Sunday*
Métro: *5, 10 Gare d'Austerlitz*   **Map:** *2*
Approximate price: *100F*

Thé des Brumes
340 rue Saint-Jacques
Tel: 43.26.35.07

What a pleasant surprise it is in this rather gloomy part of the rue Saint-Jacques, not far from the boulevard de Port-Royal, to discover, between a greengrocer and a laundry, a small, well-lit, tastefully decorated establishment, more of a tea room than a restaurant, taking into account the extra opening hours, between four and six in the afternoon. The sign is appropriately shaped like a tea-pot. And you can sample about twenty different varieties of tea here, some of them scented and none in tea-bags. There are also a number of rather uncommon, carefully prepared dishes.

You are under no obligation to order an entrée, main course and dessert here, so you can make do with just one dish, like many of the young staff of the nearby Val-de-Grâce hospital or publishing houses in the vicinity who come here to have a bite to eat during their lunch hour.

But it is certainly worth going through all the courses described on the attractively handwritten bill of fare: seven or eight entrées, three salads, three main dishes, vegetable tart, oven-browned dishes *(gratins)*, various cheese arrangements, and six desserts. The food is by no means purely vegetarian: the *salade complète* (50F), for instance, is composed of crushed wheat grains, ham, cheese, cucumbers, tomatoes, sweet peppers, green salad and walnuts, while the *salade nordique* (52F) includes smoked salmon from Norway. **Thé des Brumes** is not the place to go if you are in the mood for a steak, however.

The house aperitif (24F), *vin Hypocras aux épices,* is a red wine seasoned with a whole gamut of spices according to a recipe dating back to the Middle Ages. Ingredients include aniseed, cloves, cinnamon, ginger, cardamom, and honey. The *patronne,* Madame Cécile, declined to divulge her personal recipe but her brew may well be worth trying.

I started out with a green salad with three small goat cheeses *(crottins)* for 50F: a generous helping of lettuce, warm cheeses, carefully prepared in the tiny kitchen separated by a thin partition from the ten or twelve small tables in the cosy dining area.

I continued with a *flan d'épinards et champignons à la menthe* (42F), a kind of potato tart with spinach, mushrooms and chopped mint leaves – quite tasty and nourishing. Fresh, cool Gamay wine from Touraine-Mesland for 66F a bottle was an appropriate companion. Other options: Saumur-Champigny "Bruyères" or Chinon "Roncée", both red wines from the Loire valley, and each costing 80F a bottle (42F for a half bottle).

To conclude my meal, I chose a wedge of the strawberry and rhubarb tart (26F) which was displayed on a small table near the entrance and had caught my eye when I came in. It turned out to be a masterpiece: a very thin crust and an unbelievably delicate flavour.

The general atmosphere here is enhanced by pleasant low-volume classical music and the lively but subdued conversations of the other guests.

A cup of coffee *pur arabica* (9F) formed the final stage of a very pleasant, light meal. I could have chosen a cinnamon, vanilla or cardamom-flavoured coffee at 12F instead.

In the afternoon, during tea time, there are two *"formulae"*, one for 35F including a choice of tea and toast with butter, jam, lemon curd or cinnamon, and one for 40F with tea and scones.

Also not to be forgotten: natural apple juice with or without spices for 6F and 14F respectively, plus a range of home-made fresh vegetable and fruit juices (carrot, orange, grapefruit, lemon, apple) for 22F.

A special feature reflecting the name of the place, a pun on the title of the famous 1938 movie starring Jean Gabin and Michèle Morgan (*"Quai des Brumes"*), is a cocktail made of lime-juice, cane sugar and white rum and called *"T'a d'beaux yeux, tu sais . . ."*, Gabin's immortal line that just about every Frenchman even nowadays remembers. And so other *"cocktails pour cinéphiles"* are named after memorable lines from films such as *"Hôtel du Nord"*, *"La Guerre des Boutons"*, and so on.

Pure malt whisky and *rhum blanc* Lamanny are available at 32F and there is an excellent beer from northern France called Jenlain which costs 15F a 25cl bottle and 40F a large bottle containing 75cl.

This very attractive little place was opened in 1983 and I hope it has a long and prosperous future.

I specially appreciated: the lovingly and expertly prepared dishes, the quiet, relaxed atmosphere, the friendly *patronne*, and the exquisite fruit tart.

Open: *From 10 am to 10 pm, 4 pm on Saturday*
Closed: *Sunday*
Métro: *13 Port-Royal*   **Map:** *2*
Approximate price: *190F*
Tea fixed price: *35-40F*

Le Tiburce
28 rue du Dragon
Tel: 45.48.57.89.

Robert Courtine's enthusiastic report in *Le Monde* on this small establishment in the rue du Dragon (between the boulevard Saint-Germain and the carrefour de la Croix-Rouge) came back to my mind when I was strolling through this narrow street around ten o'clock one night not quite knowing where I might still be able to dine decently and appropriately at that hour.

The bill of fare posted at the entrance of **Le Tiburce** was advertising a menu for 125F composed of *salade de boeuf* (beef salad) or *crudités* (raw vegetables) or *oeufs en meurette* (a typical Burgundian dish of poached eggs in a red wine sauce) as entrées, poultry (*volaille*) or an *andouillette au vin blanc* (chitterling sausage cooked in white wine) as main dishes and a choice of *profiteroles au chocolat, crème caramel* and *pruneaux au vin* (prunes stewed in wine) as desserts.

This seemed inviting enough for me to enter the restaurant without any further hesitation and take a seat at a table covered with a white linen cloth. In the oblong dining room with alternating round and rectangular tables surrounded by chairs (no benches here for a change!) there is room for about forty people. Paintings by contemporary artists ornament the walls. A beautiful bouquet of flowers sits on the buffet in the back. Although not really crowded, a good many tables are still occupied on this late

Monday evening and the background noise from the conversation sounds lively without being disturbing. The dishes are carefully prepared and agreeably served on porcelain plates decorated with a red floral pattern, brought by a quiet, very attentive and conscientious waitress. The thick *andouillette* (65F à la carte) which follows the *oeufs en meurette* (50F) is sprinkled with finely chopped shallots and fresh parsley and garnished with small fried potatoes.

The linen napkins and the heavy cutlery increased my confidence, and the beautifully-shaped, large wine glasses and an impressive selection of Burgundies on the wine list persuaded me to order a half bottle of 1979 Santenay, produced and bottled by the wine growers Philippe Chapel et Fils at Santenay for 85F. Unfortunately, the wine, while being round, full-bodied and quite heavy, did not seem as subtle as I had hoped. I had, on another occasion, a similar experience with their 1987 red Chassagne-Montrachet (200F a bottle, 112F a half bottle). A less pretentious and more satisfying choice is perhaps the Touraine-Mesland, a small red Loire wine from the Cabernet Franc grape made by Girault-Artois at Mesland and served at 60F the bottle and 42F the carafe.

To give a more extensive idea of the repertoire at **Le Tiburce** the *plats du jour* on one particular spring day included *coquilles Saint-Jacques* (scallops) *nature* or *à la provençale* (160F) and *rognon de veau* (calf's kidney) *grillé* or *à la Bourgogne* (98F).

The simple, attractively priced menu which honours the promise of *"specialités bourguignonnes"*, is complemented by the bill of fare which includes dishes like six *escargots bourguignons* (snails) for 50F, two *fonds d'artichaut frais* for 45F, a *canard au poivre vert* (duck with green peppers) for 78F, and *onglet aux échalotes* (rib of beef with shallots) for 75F, and a *plateau de fromages* (cheese platter) for 45F.

The service is perfect, the atmosphere comfortably relaxed, the plates are generously filled with good, well-prepared food. After I had finished my meal the amiable waitress came to my table asking whether I would like "a little coffee" and, after my affirmative answer, first brought some sugar and an empty cup which she filled, on her second round, with deliciously smelling, steaming hot black coffee.

I have retained fond memories of this small comfortable restaurant in the quiet rue du Dragon barely two hundred yards from the busy boulevard Saint-Germain overflowing with tourists.

Open: *Orders taken until 10.15 pm. Open in August*
Closed: *Sunday and every other Saturday. The last 15 days in July*
Métro: *4 Saint-Sulpice*   **Map:** *2*
Approximate price: *200F*

Chez Toutoune
5 rue de Pontoise
Tel: 43. 26. 56. 81.

Chez Toutoune in the rue de Pontoise, a small street between the Seine and the boulevard Saint-Germain, is another restaurant with that unmistakable accent on regional dishes which, besides an emphasis on traditional food from *cuisine bourgeoise* is the distinctive mark of the restaurants selected for this guide.

Here, too, as at **Au Petit Tonneau** (page 76), it is a woman who is running things, the blonde, amiable *Provençale* Colette Dejean. In the spacious dining room seating about seventy people at some fifteen tables, *la toutoune*, as she is sometimes called, acts as hostess escorting newcomers to their table, taking their orders, explaining dishes where necessary and advising guests when asked, in a charming, patient manner, and very knowledgeably.

There is a fixed-price menu at 168.50F always including a tureen of good soup to start with, such a reassuring old French custom that regrettably has begun to disappear nowadays, followed by one of five or six entrées and a choice of as many main dishes plus two or three sorts of cheese (Brie de Meaux, *tomme*, Saint-Nectaire . . .) or one of three or four desserts such as *oeufs au lait, oeufs à la neige, mousse au chocolat, tarte maison* . . .

On an arbitrary weekday – the place is closed on Sunday (and Monday at midday) – entrées chalked on a large blackboard above the service counter include *le papeton d'aubergine au coulis de tomate* and *le tian de morue*. The first is an Avignon speciality of aubergines puréed with eggs and olive oil, baked in a dish originally shaped like the papal tiara (which accounts for its name) and served in a light fresh tomato sauce. This dish was invented during the papal exile in Avignon in the fourteenth century by local cooks who succeeded in charming the Pope's palate to such an extent that he preferred it to the creations of his own Italian cooks. The story adds interest to this centuries-old *provençal* dish, one of the many classic aubergine-tomato combinations.

Le tian de morue is another typically *provençal* recipe. A *tian* is a large, shallow, rectangular earthenware dish used to bake *au gratin*. The *tian de morue*, is a gratin made from dried, salted cod and a speciality from Carpentras, a town about thirty-five kilometres north-east of Avignon: chopped cooked spinach with leek, parsley, purslane (a spicy herb), garlic, nutmeg, eggs, anchovy fillets and milk at the bottom of the *tian* is then covered with a layer of salt cod which, in turn, is covered with another layer of the vegetable mixture topped off with breadcrumbs and olive oil.

On another day, you may find *tabboulé* on offer, a salad of coarsely ground semolina (such as that used in *couscous*) soaked with tomatoes, and garnished and seasoned with onion, fresh mint, and lots of lemon juice. Or there might be *tapenade*, a paste of capers (for which the *provençal* word is *tapena*), fillets of anchovy, crushed black olives (the small niçois variety), olive oil, lemon juice and herbs, served with raw vegetables such as celery, fennel, tomatoes, cucumbers, sweet peppers . . . .

There are a lot more southern French specialities of which you might not know the names, which appear from time to time on **Chez Toutoune**'s blackboard. Don't hesitate to ask Madame Dejean to explain to you such delicacies as *sanguette*, *"un mets de roi"*, a royal dish, according to the late Lyonnais master-chef Alain Chapel. She seems to like to puzzle people or arouse their curiosity by such terms as *truffes du Canada* for Jerusalem artichokes or *sauce chien* (literally: dog sauce) for a sharp vinaigrette from the West Indies, spiced with red hot peppers and onions.

Another attraction at **Chez Toutoune** is the *poisson du marché,* a dish of fresh fish from the fish market on the other side of the boulevard Saint-Germain. Take as examples a *petite daurade aux pommes de terre au thym:* a small sea bream with thyme-scented potatoes, or a *navarin de poissons*, a ragout of various sea fish with vegetables. I found the *choucroute de poissons*, creamy sauerkraut cooked in fish broth with whelks and fresh cod that I had on a recent Saturday afternoon, a real delight. A different fish dish appears every day, always prepared inventively from fresh produce.

Sometimes the famous *provençal* speciality *brandade de morue*, a purée of dried salt cod with lots of good olive oil (about half a litre to a kilo of fish), some milk and garlic, painstakingly and continuously stirred with a wooden ladle (the *provençal* word *brandar* means just that) is available too.

Knowing about the crowds that usually invade **Chez Toutoune**, especially on Saturday nights (the place is much more quiet at midday) I had booked well in advance in order to be sure of admission to the fairy-tale realm of Toutoune's *cuisine* and her charming personality. Lo and behold: the bill of fare featured an entrée with *aioli*, a thick mayonnaise of fresh egg yolks and fruity olive oil with lots of fresh, crushed garlic, the national pride of Provence.

An invitingly large quantity of whelks *(bulots)* fished on the Normandy coast and arriving fresh every day (except Monday) in Paris markets, was brought to my table to be dipped in the hearty *aioli*, a wonderful appetizer. It was accompanied by the refreshing young white Sauvignon from the good grower Henri Marionnet in the eastern Touraine region available here at 95F a bottle. The wine can alternatively be replaced by a half bottle of equally young Bourgogne Aligoté for 43F or by a whole or half-bottle of the reputed Pouilly Fumé from the grower Ladoucette for 162F or 86F, respectively.

The main dish, an earthenware vessel with oven-browned creamy *brandade de morue* was accompanied by a bottle of 1987 Saint-Nicolas-de-Bourgeuil of Christian Provin which was not bad but left no appreciable trace in my memory. It was the only red Loire wine available that day. There is a selection of fourteen red Bordeaux wines for between 80 and 240F.

The *brandade* was a delight in which the fish, olive oil, and garlic were harmoniously combined. Harmony was the characteristic feature of the whole meal which I concluded with a light, airy *île flottante*, (caramelised soft meringue on a vanilla custard).

If you can, try to come at midday, it is much less crowded and noisy than at night, and you have a better chance of appreciating the special charm and atmosphere of the spacious dining room with its changing exhibition of contemporary paintings.

And try the home-made *andouillette à la ficelle* (chitterling sausage) approved by the *Association Amicale des Amateurs d'Authentiques Andouillettes (A.A.A.A.A.)* available at 90F *à la carte*. You could have the soup tureen *(soupière)* for 35F, one of the set menu's entrées at 42F and a dessert at 40F which would bring the price of your meal to 207F.

The *andouillette A.A.A.A.A.* is also available to take away at **La Toutoune Gourmande**, the delicatessen store next door to the restaurant at 7 rue de Pontoise (Tel: 43.25.35.93) which might be worth a visit for other goodies too. It is open seven days a week.

Open: *12 to 2 pm and 7.45 to 10.45 pm*
Closed: *Sunday all day, and Monday at midday*
Métro: *10 Maubert Mutualité*   **Map:** *2*
Approximate price: *240F*
Fixed-price menu: *168.50F*

Chez René
10 boulevard Saint-Germain
Tel: 43.54.30.23

Although the clientèle is still mainly French with quite a few local regulars populating **Chez René**'s bistro dining room on the boulevard Saint-Germain where it crosses the rue du Cardinal-Lemoine, an increasing number of foreign visitors now find their way to this still thoroughly French bistro.

This does not always help to maintain standards. On one of my latest visits I detected signs of fatigue in some of the cooking (the *saucisson chaud*, for instance, was not of the utmost freshness, the *haricot de mouton*, a stew of mutton in tomatoed white haricot beans, was a bit flabby and contained more bones than meat . . .). But it is an extremely rare restaurant that never slips, and I have had enough impeccable meals at **René**'s to keep coming back and to recommend this small refuge of authenticity and generosity on the boundaries of the Latin Quarter. It is difficult to find good, unadulterated and still affordable bistro fare around here.

I usually start my meal with a glass of cool white wine as an aperitif. The Mâcon-Viré (80F a bottle) is spicy and concentrated and costs 14F a well-filled glass. Another option would be the fresh, fruity Sauvignon de Touraine from grower Jean-Marie Penet at Oisly at 52F a bottle.

A good entrée option is the *assiette de cochonnailles* (50F), consisting of various sorts of cold sliced sausages and hams. The *saucisson chaud* (sliced hot pork sausage with a superb warm potato salad – 50F), too, is usually excellent for entrée. But there is also a refreshing, slightly bitter *salade de mesclun* (28F), a mixed salad of all sorts of young green leaves, usually including cress, lamb's lettuce, young dandelion leaves, fennel, chervil, purslane (a fragrant, succulent herb, less known in Britain) and other herbs most of which were originally found wild in Provence where the recipe and the name *mesclun* (meaning "mixed") also come from.

Main dishes I have enjoyed at **René**'s include *gras double* (78F), a well-spiced stew of beef tripe and calf's foot, served steaming hot and giving off a beautifully appetizing scent, *coq au vin* (chicken in red wine with onions, mushrooms and bacon – 82F), *andouillette au vin blanc* (chitterling sausage braised in white wine – 64F), and *boudin du pays "pommes en l'air"* (country-style black pudding with apples – 64F).

The traditional *gâteau de riz* (cold, caramelised rice pudding) served with a raspberry-flavoured vanilla custard, is a little clammy at times but there are another twenty desserts available including fresh pastries, tarts, charlottes, *crème caramel*. Ice cream called *bouchon de fine champagne*, shaped like a Champagne cork with good Cognac (Fine Champagne) poured over, costs about 35F, while wild strawberries or raspberries with sugar or in wine or with cream can be had for 62F.

But before embarking on a dessert, don't miss out on the magnificent cheese platter (37F) which comes together with another smaller *plateau* with ping-pong ball sized cylindrical goat's cheeses.

Wine comes from the *patron's* own family vineyards around Emeringes in the Beaujolais. The generic Beaujolais is full-bodied but lacks acidity, a typical flaw in the 1989 vintage (the vines had too much sun). Its price, 68F, is very reasonable. The Chénas, one of the *crus* of the Beaujolais (90F), also comes from the Cinquin's property. And so does a 1988 Juliénas at the same price which was rather popular with the regulars when I last ate here.

René's son, Monsieur Jean-Paul Cinquin, the bistro's present owner, attentively watches the proceedings in the L-shaped dining room from the centrally-located service counter. The expert service is carried out by a team of experienced waiters in black waistcoats and long aprons who greet the regulars by name, all this providing an authentic background that breathes solidity and timelessness.

At the exit, a number of photographs of this old restaurant at different periods adorn the walls on both sides of the door.

Open: 12.15 to 2.15 pm and 7.45 to 10.15 pm
Closed: Saturday and Sunday
Métro: 10 Cardinal-Lemoine   *Map:* 2
Approximate price: 250F

Au Gourmet de l'Isle
42 rue Saint-Louis-en-Ile
Tel: 43.26.79.27

The old, familiar "Chez Bourdeau" signboard on this ancient building between a bread and pastry shop and a butcher's, on the quaintly old-fashioned Ile St Louis, has disappeared. Jules Bourdeau who ran this restaurant for more than sixty-five years retired in 1988 (at an age far above eighty – he was then the oldest restaurant keeper in Paris), and from June of that year, Jean-Michel Mestivier, a co-owner, officiates in the kitchen.

In the oblong dining room, flanked by benches on either side with solid wooden tables and chairs along them, I recently had a pleasant Sunday lunch to see if the quality of the food was up to the old standards.

The prices have hardly changed in the past three years. The set four-course menu is still only 110F (a mere ten franc mark-up in more than three years!) and offers a choice of ten entrées, seven main courses, a cheese platter or a salad, and fourteen desserts. That is the whole bill of fare on which entrées, salad and desserts are all marked 28F, while main dishes cost 57F, with the exception of the *faux filet grillé à l'échalote* (grilled sirloin with shallots) which is 75F.

As most of the dishes on the menu were still the same as they had been for decades under Monsieur Bourdeau's reign, I was very curious to learn what had really changed.

By force of habit, I took the *fond d'artichaut frais Saint-Louis,* a house speciality of old, as entrée, and found that there was only one fresh artichoke heart (instead of two as before) and the poached egg had been replaced by a hard-boiled egg, the latter substitution being an accident, I was assured when I asked later. The accompanying *gribiche* sauce (with fresh herbs and capers), however, was as delicious and smooth as ever.

Other entrées include *tête de veau rémoulade* (head of veal), salad of boiled beef with green lentils from the Auvergne, and *oeufs en meurette* (poached eggs in a red wine sauce with bacon).

I chose a pot-roasted *andouillette* translated as "tripe sausage with kidney beans in wine" on the English menu (the bill of fare is also in Italian and Spanish) which was to my entire satisfaction.

For accompaniment I chose a bottle of Marcillac (50F) from the Cave des Vignerons du Vallon at Valady in Aveyron which is a perfect companion to the simple, generous country fare on offer here. Don't hesitate to ask for a bucket of ice water to cool it down if you find it too warm. Other wine options include a Côtes-de-Bourg Château Moulin-de-la-Marzelle, and a Chinon, a Bourgeuil and a red Saumur from the Loire, all for well under 100F.

The house speciality is *la charbonnée de l'Isle au marcillac,* pork in red wine with bacon, baby onions and *croûtons*, served with two large boiled potatoes. Other interesting main dishes from *cuisine bourgeoise*: brains (calf's or lamb's) with melted butter and boiled potatoes, and sautéd lamb's sweetbreads with spinach leaves (*épinards en branche*).

The cheese platter offers four cheeses among which are *fourme* d'Ambert and Camembert.

I enjoyed the salad of chicory with walnuts and was glad there was a salt shaker and a pepper mill at hand on the linen-covered table to adjust its seasoning. Salad instead of cheese is sometimes a welcome variation, especially when the main course has been rich. Too few Paris restaurants offer this traditional alternative.

For dessert I enjoyed the pears in red Marcillac wine. Other possibilities: fresh cream cheese with raisins, pastries and various ice creams and sorbets.

Cona coffee (12F) comes in white conical porcelain mugs. As it is not always freshly made, I avoid it most of the time.

Quite remarkably, the change of ownership has not appreciably impaired the time-honoured style and the quality of the fare in this traditional restaurant on the extremely tourist-ridden Ile St Louis and I am pleased that I can still recommend this Parisian land-mark warmly.

There was good company, mainly regulars of all ages, the Sunday I was last there, and the service was correctly carried out by an informally dressed young waiter.

There is another large dining room in the basement which I found less attractive than the ground floor because of the cramped and rather noisy atmosphere. A thing to remember when booking.

Open: *12 pm to 2 pm and 7 pm to 10 pm*
Closed: *Monday and Tuesday*
Métro: *7 Pont Marie*   **Map:** *2*
Approximate price: *160*
Fixed-price menu: *120F*

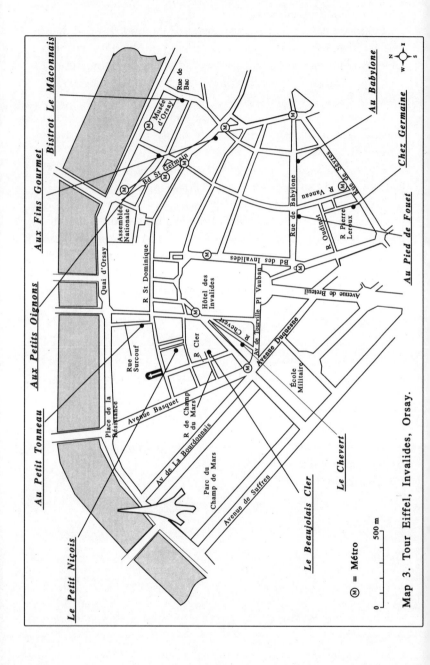

Map 3. Tour Eiffel, Invalides, Orsay.

Ⓜ = Métro

Tour Eiffel, Invalides, Orsay

Arrondissement 7

Au Babylone
13 rue de Babylone
Tel: 45.48.72.13

Behind the huge – and by no means inexpensive – department store with the misleading name *Au Bon Marché*, in the somewhat gloomy rue de Babylone you will find a quaint, small and rather inexpensive restaurant.

Entering by the glass door, you find on the left a curve of four tables alongside a long bench, and on the right a marble-covered *zinc* with an antique telephone and a modern espresso machine. Behind this there is a long, narrow dining room with pans, plates, paintings and red-shaded lamps on the yellow walls, a large mirror in the back and a pigeonhole rack with the red cotton napkins for the *habitués* next to the kitchen door.

A young, efficient waitress and a *garçon* clad in blue jeans and a T-shirt take the orders and bring the plates and carafes. The bill of fare, handwritten each day, as in so many of this type of little neighbourhood restaurant, is simple and lucid. Hors d'oeuvre like *carottes rapées, radis beurre, rillettes, tomates en salade,* etcetera, at 11F or 13F, about five main dishes like *poulet rôti, gigot d'agneau, rosbief* for 39F or 40F, a few standard desserts and cheeses (Gruyère, Cantal, Camembert, bleu d'Auvergne, Saint Nectaire) for 11F. The *tarte aux poires* (pear tart) is 15F and side dishes of green salad, mashed potatoes, flageolet beans and chicory are available at 7F.

The day I ate there, *gras double* (a succulent dish of stewed beef tripe with boiled potatoes) was on the menu and much sought after by regulars, so it was doubtless good – it certainly looked and smelled attractive.

I had calf's liver, a good-sized slice sprinkled with fresh parsley, on a small plate filled to the brim with creamy mashed potatoes and well-flavoured sauce (40F), after savouring a slice of country *pâté basque* (15F), carefully presented with good pickled gherkin. The 23cl carafe of Côtes-de-Provence (11F) was to my liking and so was the *gâteau aux pruneaux* that arrived on my table for dessert: prunes with a warm vanilla cream between two layers of pastry.

Following an old peasant custom, the wine is sometimes diluted with fresh water by those who want to avoid getting sleepy in the afternoon. Fresh water, of course, is always brought to the table automatically in pitchers and mineral water (Vittel, Badoit) is available in bottles at 7F. French beer costs 8F and Heineken 12F.

My offer to have my cup of coffee (6F) at the *zinc* to make room for new arrivals (the place was filled to capacity) is firmly refused in a friendly manner by the resolute waitress, *"C'est mieux pour vous à la table"*, you will enjoy it more at your table. And that's the way it was.

Thirty minutes after I had arrived, I was standing outside again after having paid a bill amounting to less than 90F: happy, invigorated, and with an optimistic outlook on life.

A typically old-fashioned Parisian restaurant, **Au Babylone** rejoices in everything in harmony: the décor, smells, atmosphere, clientèle, prices and the expertise and care bestowed on the preparation of the food. And, what is certainly not to be forgotten: that indispensable link between host and guest which is provided by the people who are serving you: firm, efficient, with a personal touch, always cordial – in short: *bon enfant*, as they say in Paris, or *anticommercial mais pur et dur*, as a nice French tourist put it when divulging this address to me.

Closed: *Every night and Sunday all day*
Métro: *10, 12 Sèvres Babylone*   **Map:** *3*
Approximate price: *85F*
No reservations

Le Beaujolais Cler

38 rue Cler
Tel: 47.05.51.27

Here, at the gleamingly polished copper *zinc* or at one of the simple formica tables, in the company of street market traders in their white or green jackets, you can drink a young Saint-Amour from a handsome large balloon glass for about 8F. That is the price at the counter. If you wish to take your wine and sit down to drink it, you will be charged one franc extra. An ordinary Beaujolais is a few francs less (6.50/7.50F) and is available either from the cool basin right under the counter or, even cooler, directly from the refrigerator.

While friendly, mustachioed Jean-Pierre busies himself behind the counter, Madame Benoît, the *patronne*, will prepare a foot-length of French bread for you with *rillettes* (minced pork cooked in its own fat). *Jambon de Paris* (slices of cooked ham), *pâté* and Camembert are available too for 10F or thereabouts. An *omelette nature* or a couple of fried eggs cost 15F (18F with ham or cheese) and an *assiette anglaise* (an assortment of *charcuterie*) can be had for less than 30F.

Apart from the two Beaujolais wines mentioned, a white Pouilly Fumé from the grower Marcel Langoux at Pouilly-sur-Loire left a lasting impression on account of its full, harmonious taste (9.50/11.50F). Very nice with a hard-boiled egg (about 3F). There is also a good Sancerre from the growers Cheaumeau and Balland at Bué (9/11F).

A short distance to the west of the Loire villages of Pouilly and Sancerre lies the region where the Cheverny wines originate. The red Cheverny from the Gamay grape (the variety from which red Beaujolais wines are made) is on offer for about 5F per 7 cl, while the fresh, cool Sauvignon from the same region (and the same grower, Gilbert Oury at Fougères-sur-Bièvre) costs a few *centimes* more. Perhaps a good companion for . . . well for what? Because food is not really the main attraction here. The quality is good but the choice is limited. There is, however, something besides the excellent quality of the wine and the authentic ambience and *clientèle* which makes the establishment worthwhile: you can eat oysters here, unceremoniously, and for comparatively little money.

Outside the café on the corner of the rue Cler and the rue du Champs-de-Mars, in between market stalls, greengrocers, fishmongers and delicatessens, every day except Monday Jean-Luc stands with his boxes and baskets full of various sorts of oysters. Prices range between 45F and just over 100F per dozen, depending on type and size (the flat Belons are the most expensive). You make your choice outside at Jean-Luc's stall, and he will open your oysters for you, arrange them carefully on a platter and carry them inside. On a table, a bottle of aromatic wine vinegar with shallots, half a lemon and a basket of bread are all ready for you (the extra cover charge is only 15F). I had one or two glasses of the splendid Pouilly Fumé with my oysters.

Everything is relaxed and informal here. This is how I imagine that oysters have always been eaten on the coasts of Brittany, Normandy or Aquitaine: simple popular food.

Cherished memories of the old Paris food market, Les Halles (moved out in 1968) are brought back to life by this wine bistro. In the heart of the busy street market between the rue de Grenelle and the avenue de la Motte-Picquet, it provides a true-to-life resurrection of the old Les Halles, be it on a much smaller scale. Whoever wants to inhale that atmosphere once more should come to the rue Cler, to **Le Beaujolais**, rather than go to such establishments as the over-famous **Au Pied de Cochon** on the rue Coquillière which has degenerated into a make-believe bistro-museum.

Open: 7.30 am to 9 pm; 7.30 am to 3 pm on Sunday
Closed: Sunday evening and Monday all day
Métro: 8 Ecole Militaire or 8 La Tour Mauboug **Map:** 3
Approximate price: 65F
No reservations

Le Chevert (Auberge Comtoise)
34 rue Chevert
Tel: 47.05.51.09

The rue Chevert is a quiet street between the boulevard de La Tour-Maubourg and the avenue de Tourville which houses just one other establishment of interest to travellers and tourists besides the **Auberge Comtoise** that carries the street's name: the solid two-star hotel **Muguet** at number 11 (Tel: 47.05.05.93). From this and the numerous other hotels in this district, many guests come to **Le Chevert**, especially in the evening, to be pampered in this country *auberge* decorated with all sorts of typical items from the Franche Comté where the recipes and ingredients of most of the dishes on offer also have their origin.

On the Friday afternoon that I walked in without having booked, the busy waitress smilingly showed me to the only unoccupied chair in the place at the table of a friendly young man who, like most of the guests at lunch, turned out to be working in the neighbourhood.

There is a fixed-price menu which, for a very modest 98F, gives you a choice between four entrées: *velouté* (soup), *tomates en salade*, *saucisson sec* (air-dried sausage), and *brési* (a regional speciality from the Franche Comté: cured, smoked and air-dried fillet of beef served in wafer-thin slices). There are also two main dishes such as *tripes à la comtoise* (tripe cooked in Arbois wine with bacon and brandy made from Arbois wine grapes), grilled pork, home-made *cassoulet* (casserole of different meats with white haricot beans), a *plateau* with three kinds of regional cheese or a wedge of one of the home-made tarts or ice cream, and a quarter of a litre of red, white or *rosé* Arbois wine served in a wooden pitcher.

The tables under the old black wooden beams on the ceiling are covered with grey-blue cotton tablecloths and napkins.

I chose the simple tomato salad which was prepared to order on a plate filled to the brim behind the wooden counter, fresh, sun-ripened tomatoes with a carefully prepared dressing and fresh green herbs. Thereafter, the friendly and efficient waitress brought a *sauté de veau* in a tastily seasoned white wine sauce and accompanied by creamy mashed potatoes.

During the meal, the *patron*, Monsieur Michel Laroche, is continually busy passing plates from the kitchen to the waitress, pouring wine for the guests and picking up empty plates from the tables here and there – there are about forty-five guests and one waitress. He still takes the trouble of coming over to me to tell me that he was sorry that I could not have a table to myself. Quite unnecessary: I was feeling at home already. Three gentlemen at an adjoining table are savouring plates full of assorted *charcuterie* – the *terrine maison* (42F) seems to be of particular interest – mysterious aromatically steaming dishes, cheese, tarts and various wines while conversing in a lively way on subjects of a political or philosophical nature. A combination which is so distinctly typical of a good Parisian meal that I always find it reassuring to witness.

It is hardly necessary to attract the waitress's attention when you are ready for cheese or dessert. The cheese platter is brought to my table promptly and I ask for a bite-sized piece of each of the three Comté cheeses. In spite of my protests three rather voluminous hunks are placed on my plate and each cheese has its own flavour and texture, and they are all so delicious that not one bit is left. The selection on offer at my most recent visit was Cancoillotte, a preparation of hard, rather grainy cheese with spices and white wine, Mamirolle, a soft, rather spicy local cheese (Mamirolle is a small town near Besançon) and bleu de Gex, all made of cow's milk.

The wine I had chosen with the main course goes very well with the cheese, too, a fruity red 1988 Côtes-du-Ventoux, sold under the name of La Vieille Ferme, at 18F a quarter of a litre, and 34F a half-litre. The *gâteau franc-comtois* is a tart with a thin layer of dough covered with a layer of bilberries and topped with a creamy mousse made of fresh white cheese and lightly sour cream glazed with a brown caramelized crust.

A cup of coffee (7F) and a glass of cold water from a carafe formed the final point of my meal, one of the best I have had in Paris.

Don't fail to notice the paintings, water colours and photographs placed here and there on the walls and all originating from the *patron*'s native region, the Franche Comté. And, above all, if you appreciate the authentic fare issuing from the kitchen, prepared by Madame Suzanne and her son Michel, you get the feeling that a meal in this place alone has been worth your trip to Paris.

In order to excite your curiosity even further, here are a few more examples from the long list of specialities on offer. The *coq au vin jaune* (88F) is chicken cooked in a rare, concentrated yellow Arbois wine, matured a minimum of six years in wooden casks; the wine can also be sampled in a 10cl glass for 52F. If you accompany the cheese (30F) with a glass of this wine, its price will only go up by 36F (66F for the cheese with the wine). The *oeufs à la comtoise* (38F), a possible first course, are eggs scrambled with

Comté cheese and small dried mushrooms. Another regional entrée you might want to sample is the *tourte franche comtoise* (40F), a meat pie of pork and veal marinated in white Arbois wine with short pastry.

Open: *Orders taken until 9.30 pm*
Closed: *Saturday and Sunday*
Métro: *8 École Militaire*   **Map:** *3*
Approximate price: *110F*
Fixed-price menu: *98F*

Aux Fins Gourmets
213 boulevard Saint-Germain
Tel: 42.22.06.57

This venerable restaurant is located in the quieter stretch of the boulevard Saint-Germain street scene, where the boulevard Raspail runs into the boulevard Saint-Germain at the junction with the rue du Bac. During a memorable meal here with Jean-Pierre Imbach, I got to know the exceptional qualities of this restaurant, which features regional dishes from the Basque and Béarnaise provinces on the western slopes of the Pyrenees. The newly-renovated canopy which covers a small terrace lined with green plants, advertises these *"Spécialités Basques et Béarnaises"*, while the interior of the bistro exhibits an unchanging and fashion-proof simplicity. The benches along the walls of the oblong dining room, backed by brass rods behind which you can put your bag, umbrella, briefcase, or whatever other paraphernalia you might wish to keep within easy reach, are comfortable and inviting. The décor, although sober, is not without a certain charm.

The aperitif, not a *kir royal* (not infrequently made with very mediocre Champagne) is a really royal *kir*, made with good dry white wine, an appropriate introduction to the abundant platter of *jambon de Bayonne* (raw ham) country *pâtés*, thin slices of *andouille* (a deliciously smoked cold chitterling sausage), and the *saucisson sec* (air-dried sausage) served as entrée (30F). I can also recommend a glass of the excellent, rich, velvety, young, dry white Jurançon (A.O.C.) for the same price as the *kir* (14F).

On my first visit, I continued with the famous *cassoulet*, a speciality of this restaurant, run by the Dupleix family for several generations. The present owner's mother, who did the cooking here for more than twenty years, and who died in 1987, has managed to transfer her know-how and skill to the present kitchen staff who still serve her delicate *cassoulet*, a sizzling earthenware casserole of white haricot beans, mutton, preserved goose (*confit d'oie*) and three different sausages, for the surprisingly low price of 77F. Apart from the renowned *cassoulet*, the bill of fare lists simple classic dishes such as *haricot de mouton* (mutton stew – 64F), *petit salé aux choux* (salt pork with cabbage – 62F), *caneton aux navets* (duckling with turnips – 61F).

The desserts, such as *pêche Melba* or *pruneaux à l'armagnac* (prunes in Armagnac), *poire belle Hélène* (poached pear with vanilla ice cream and hot chocolate sauce) are carefully prepared, generously presented and well flavoured, and priced between 19F and 25F.

Coffee here is not espresso, but *café cona* which might be a welcome bonus for people who like their coffee less strong than is customary in French restaurants. Of whatever type, coffee is an appropriate final touch to a copious meal accompanied by a robust, deep red wine from the Pyrenees called Madiran (A.O.C.), the pronounced flavour of which harmonises perfectly with the hearty fare from the Dupleix kitchen. Madiran, made from Tannat, Cabernet Franc and Fer grapes, and matured for more than a year in wooden casks, has sometimes been compared to Burgundy, probably because of its relatively long maturation and its special appropriateness as an accompaniment to venison and roast meat. All sorts of health claims have been made for Madiran wine, but then, to my mind, any honest wine is healthy. As an old French author is reported to have said, *"Le vin est comme le médecin: il guérit parfois, il soulage souvent, il console toujours"* (Wine is like the physician: sometimes it will cure, often it will soothe, but it will always console).

A country bistro like **Aux Fins Gourmets**, right in the heart of Paris, cherished by editors and writers from neighbouring publishing houses, by members of the adjacent National Assembly and, last but not least, by many an anonymous gourmet, deserves attention.

I specially appreciated: the country *charcuterie*, *cassoulet*, Madiran wine, relaxed atmosphere, and good value for money.

Closed: *Sunday all day and Monday at midday*
Métro: *12 Rue du Bac* **Map:** *3*
Approximate price: 190F

Chez Germaine
30 rue Pierre-Leroux
Tel: 42.73.28.34

In a narrow side street off the busy rue de Sèvres – there is an interesting cheese shop, *Maison de Fromage*, on the corner of the two streets – you will find on your left Madame Germaine's tiny restaurant (eight tables for four, almost on top of each other) which, without any hesitation, I would call Paris's best bistro for people with small purses and large, discerning appetites.

It was a real revelation when I first came here several years ago! There is always soup (*potage* – 6F) in the evening, a feature worth mentioning because it is very rare in Paris (other "soup places" in this guide: **La Grosse Tartine**, page 148, **Chez Toutoune**, page 48, **Au Pied de Fouet,** page 79). There is a choice of twenty entrées including simple classics such as mackerel fillets, celeriac with *remoulade* (spicy mayonnaise), *saucisson sec* (air-dried pork sausage) with butter, *crudités* (raw vegetables), *oeuf mayonnaise*, all for 8.50F, and specialities not to be found easily on a simple bistro menu, such as a *salade de fruits de mer* (seafood salad – 14F), *moules en salade à la remoulade* (mussels – 12F), *terrine aux cèpes* (boletus mushroom terrine – 10F).

Main dishes are between 2F5 and 30F (except for the *chateaubriand grillé* at 40F). These an impressive eleven in number, including pork, beef, veal, fish, liver, tripe and a house speciality, *bitoke à la russe,* which is a mixture of minced pork, veal and beef, bound with egg and breadcrumb, fried in butter and served with a tomato sauce (and spaghetti).

I started my meal with a *museau ravigote à la ciboulette*, a good slice of delicate brawn or pork muzzle jelly with a herb vinaigrette with lots of chives, and continued with *quenelles de brochet* (pike dumplings) with a crayfish sauce (*sauce Nantua*) and rice, a dish all the constituents of which had obviously been prepared on the spot, with good fresh raw materials and loving care, bearing no resemblance to insipid supermarket copies.

The *clafoutis maison*, a warm batter cake with apples and pears, is very good, like just about everything you order here. Together with a small carafe of the very drinkable house red (there is also a Bordeaux for 12.50F and a Côtes-du-Ventoux for 10F) my bill came to 52.80F.

There is no coffee and *"Madame Germaine interdit de fumer"*, says a prominently placed board, a very understandable and − considering the microscopic dimensions of the dining room − even a welcome restriction on smokers, which leaves the fragrance emanating from the various dishes intact.

It's nearly always crowded here, especially at midday, and the resolute but friendly *patronne* has her hands fully occupied with the serving of a seemingly endless supply of deliciously filled platters, while announcing at the top of her voice *"un quenelles"* towards the kitchen and *"deux personnes"* towards the entrance, where a small queue of hungrily waiting guests often forms. Try to arrive before twelve or after two o'clock.

A discovery for anyone who wants to join ordinary Parisians joyfully indulging in their everyday eating habits!

Open: *11.30 am to 2.30 pm and 6.30 to 9.00 pm*
Closed: *Saturday night and Sunday all day*
Métro: *10 Vaneau or 10, 13 Duroc*   **Map:** *3*
Approximate price: *60F*

Bistrot le Mâconnais
10 rue du Bac
Tel: 42.61.21.89

Before Pierre Lefebvre, the young, dynamic *patron* turned it into **Le Mâconnais** in 1983, this was the then well-known **Chope d'Orsay,** named after the nearby gare d'Orsay, the old railway station that has now been transformed into the Musée d'Orsay, where "all aspects of artistic achievement in the second half of the nineteenth and the beginning of the twentieth century" await the visitor.

What is awaiting the visitor in **Le Mâconnais** is first and foremost good wine from the region around Mâcon and the Beaujolais. Unfortunately, Pierre Lefebvre has recently had to discontinue serving wine by the glass at his wood-covered *zinc* because it attracted an irritating crowd in a neighbourhood that is becoming more and more thronged with tourists since the opening of the Musée d'Orsay in 1986.

On a recent visit, however, I found that a great variety of wine is still available, served by the glass or in carafes of various sizes at the table. So I was able to sample several good white wines from the Mâconnais: a delightful Mâcon-Clessé 1988 from Gilbert Mornand at 22/43/61F for 8/20/33 cl or 112F the bottle (better value). The Mâcon-Viré from another village in the Mâconnais region, made by the good local Cave Cooperative (vintage year 1988) at 20/37/54/94F, was rather stern, typically for this *appellation*, a wine with undeniable character of its own. A Saint-Véran is available at the same price as the Mâcon-Clessé, also a Beaujolais *blanc* and the prestigious Pouilly-Loché.

What a delight to have the chance to sample all these different white wines from southern Burgundy which give **Le Mâconnais** its name! A name also reflected by the selection of food listed on the bill of fare: *fricassé d'escargots* (snails – 38F), *cervelas pommes à l'huile* (saveloys, slices of sausage with potato salad – 48F), *andouillette à la ficelle sauce moutarde* (chitterling sausage with tripe cut into long strips, served with a mustard sauce – 58F), *selle d'agneau au thym* (saddle of lamb with thyme – 63F), *fromage fort*

(26F), *fromage mâconnais* (32F), *mousse au chocolat, île flottante* (28F), *tarte du jour* for about 30F.

There is a different *plat du jour* every day (calf's liver for 78F on a recent visit) and classic meat dishes such as *entrecôte marchand de vin* (red wine sauce with shallots) and *onglet à l'échalotte* (flank of beef with shallots) for 63F, while fish dishes are on offer *"selon l'arrivage"*, depending on the supply, for 64F.

Most of the dishes are served with *gratin dauphinois,* delicious oven-browned sliced potatoes cooked in milk and cream.

A few tables on the ground floor seat about twenty people, while there is room for another thirty-four upstairs. All the homely fittings of a typical bistro are there: an *étagère,* one of those light open sets of shelves with copper legs housing such paraphernalia as salt and pepper shakers, mustard pots, waiters' serviettes, etcetera, and a beautifully arranged bouquet of flowers on the marble-covered service counter.

The variety and style of this menu first brought me here with my friend and mentor, Jean-Pierre Imbach. We were shown to a small table between the *zinc* and the window near the entrance and started with an *apéritif du patron,* on that occasion a *kir* of red Beaujolais and wild blackberry liqueur, at 18F – surprisingly agreeable and refreshing. On another visit it was a white Mâcon with a liqueur of vineyard peaches.

Our memorable meal started with me relishing an *eminé d'épinards au poisson mariné* (a salad of marinated fish on a bed of crisp, par-boiled spinach leaves – 42F) while Jean-Pierre enjoyed an *assiette de charcuterie de chez Bobosse* (42F), a dish of assorted *charcuterie,* supplied by the famous *charcutier,* René Besson, alias Bobosse, from the Lyon area, who also supplies the great restaurants of Paul Bocuse and the late Alain Chapel. Chunks of braised lamb's sweetbreads in a delicate sauce with oven-browned *gratin dauphinois* potatoes were my main course, and Jean-Pierre had an excellent *fricassée de poulet à la crême* (chicken fricassée) with steamed potatoes for 58F.

We shared a bottle of red Côte-Roannaise (v.d.q.s.), made from Gamay and Pinot Noir grapes by the growers Paul-Louis Lapandery et Fils at Saint-Haon-le-Vieux in the upper Loire valley just west of the Beaujolais region. A light, fresh, aromatic wine worth remembering. On my last visit to **Le Mâconnais** it was unfortunately not available. Instead, I sampled a fruity full-bodied, well-structured 1988 Regnié, the most recently promoted tenth *cru* of the Beaujolais, expertly made by Jean-Paul Ruet at Voujon-Cercié. It costs 48F for 33 cl and 90F a bottle. Mâcon rouge costs 20F per glass, 70F a bottle, but there is also one available in a 46 cl *pot* at 34F. A *pot* is a heavy-footed bottle of thick, colourless glass popular with *pétanque* players in and around the Beaujolais region. Beaujolais-Villages, Brouilly, Chiroubles and Juliénas are available at 84F, 110F, 112F and 114F a bottle respectively.

The desserts, a *gratin de fruits de saison* (*crème d'orange* at the time – 35F), and an *île flottante* at 28F, were of the same quality as the other dishes and I have no reason to doubt that this will also be the case with the *terrine de légumes au coulis de tomate*, a vegetable terrine with tomato coulis, and the *jambon persillé* (ham in white wine jelly with parsley) for 32F, two entrées I discovered when re-examining the bill of fare.

I specially appreciated: a comparatively new wine bistro, with an accomplished and inventive kitchen using fresh ingredients, an interesting selection of wines, an efficient and friendly service executed by young waiters in white shirts and black trousers, and a very gentle and lovable *patron*. If you ask him, he will reimburse your telephone money if you book in advance! He is so anxious to spare himself the embarrassment of having to turn you away if there is no more room. Absolutely imperative to book for Saturday nights!

Open: *12 to 2.30 pm and 7 to 10.30 pm*
Closed: *Saturday at midday and Sunday all day*
Métro: *12 Rue du Bac*   **Map:**   *3*
Approximate price: *200F*

Le Petit Niçois
10 rue Amélie
Tel: 45.51.83.65

Even though one of the last authentic Paris *bougnats* (a small merchant of coal, firewood, and other combustible materials such as wine by the glass) will have disappeared from the rue Amélie in 1991, this street is still worth finding for those in search of somewhere that provides the pleasures of good food in a cosy and lively atmosphere. **Le Petit Niçois** at Number Ten is such a place.

The shining blue on the sign and the white lettering which, from a distance, vaguely looks like a foam-covered wave of the sea might induce the visitor with romantic inclinations to think of the blue skies above the wind-swept Mediterranean.

This visual attractiveness is reinforced by the good value of the excellent fare on offer inside. For the modest sum of 145F a meal is available here as a set menu consisting of three original and generous courses.

To begin with, there is a choice of eleven entrées from *beignets aubergines, moules farcies* (mussels), *salade de tomates, melon glacé* up to *asperges vinaigrette*. Among the thirteen main dishes you will find, besides *steack grillé* or *steack au poivre vert flambé* and *côtes d'agneau* (lamb chops) with *beignets d'aubergines,* dishes of salmon, sole, sardines and squid (*calamars*). And, daily, *la bouillabaisse de Nice* and *la paëlla du chef* (thirty minutes' wait for the latter).

Thereafter you can order some Cantal, Roquefort, or goat cheese. Or you can conclude your meal with one of the various ice creams or sorbets available, a *mousse au chocolat*, a *tarte du chef*, a home-made *charlotte* or one of the five other desserts on offer.

On a rather gloomy October evening around nine, when I came here for the first time, there was unfortunately no more room in the dining area at the back, and I had to make do with a small table opposite the service buffet near the entrance. But my initial disappointment at this minor inconvenience was almost immediately effaced by the arrival of a bowl of excellent *aioli*, a home-made mayonnaise with crushed raw garlic, accompanied by a dozen whelks (*bulots*). When I tried this combination together with a sip of the slightly fizzy white Gros Plant du Pays Nantais *sur lie* from the good supplier Sauvion et Fils at Vallet, and a bite of one of the three different kinds of bread (rye, sourdough and white *baguette*), I was certain that the evening would turn out to be an unmitigated pleasure.

And my confidence was confirmed by the arrival of a steaming hot bowl of *bouillabaisse de Nice:* seven kinds of fish plus various molluscs and crustaceans: the big claw of a North Sea crab, mussels, and a giant prawn among them, all bathed in an aromatic broth set down on my table, together with two soup bowls (one for the shells and other debris), a basket of *croûtons*, a small bowl of *rouille* and another with freshly grated cheese. The *rouille* is a sauce made of crushed chilli peppers (*piment*), garlic, breadcrumbs, mashed potatoes, olive oil, and sometimes some fish liver. Its name derives from its rusty colour, *rouille* being the French word for rust.

The *bouillabaisse* itself is originally a fisherman's dish based on a mixture of freshly-caught fish from the Mediterranean which, due to their ugliness or their small size, are considered unfit for normal sale, with a few small shellfish added. The fish with more solid flesh are first marinaded along with the shellfish for several hours in fruity olive oil with finely chopped onions, tomatoes and garlic, fennel, parsley, thyme, bay leaves, freshly ground pepper and, indispensably, orange peel and saffron. Then cold water is added, the mixture is boiled over a large fire for seven or eight minutes. Then the fish with lighter flesh are immersed in the liquid and the stew is simmered for another seven minutes.

In Marseille where this fish dish is said to have originated, in dozens and dozens of fish restaurants around the old fishing port, which is one of the city's major tourist attractions, you can get a dish named *bouillabaisse* for exactly the same price in each establishment. Some years ago, I ate something in one of these places that I forgot very shortly afterwards. But I still remember that it was called *bouillabaisse* and that it was not cheap (60F plus 15% service charge in 1982!).

At **Le Petit Niçois**, in 1990, the *bouillabaisse de Nice* costs 95F (including service) if you order it separately (that is to say, not as part of the set menu) and is so delicious that the memory lasts for a long time.

This is an excellent illustration of what I find to be the general situation in France. Nowadays it is easier to find typically provincial dishes, authentically prepared with fresh ingredients from their province of origin, in Paris, than it is in their indigenous region itself, especially if a region, like the French Riviera, is very popular with tourists and correspondingly adorned with an abundance of catering facilities: a network of tourist traps. And the handful of well-known "good" addresses do not really offer a way out, for, as a rule, those heavily star-spangled restaurants match their gastronomic qualities with astronomical prices, making them inaccessible to a majority of ordinary people. This is aggravated by the fact that originally simple, country dishes, when prepared in these star-decorated restaurants, are available only in "refined" or "enriched" versions like *bouillabaisse* with spiny lobster (*langoustine*) alone – a heresy far from the spirit of the original recipe.

Yet, in the authentic regional restaurants of Paris, people who are themselves originally from the region manage to prepare these dishes with loving dedication and authentic ingredients procured from local producers to whom they are often linked by family ties. Their faithful clientèle invariably includes people from the same native region who come to eat "as they did as a child at home", thus cherishing the ties with their native province.

The seven sorts of fish in the *bouillabaisse* of **Le Petit Niçois** are: first of all, of course, the indispensable *rascasse* which, however, here comes not from the Mediterranean, but from the Atlantic, which is much closer geographically. The slight inferiority in taste of the blue mouth *(rascasse atlantique)* to its Mediterranean twin brother is more than compensated for by its obvious superiority in freshness. Then: *rouget* (red mullet), *grondin* (gurnard), *congre* (conger eel), *vive* (weever), *saint-pierre* (John Dory) and *mulet* (mullet). This is what **Le Petit Niçois**' cook told me when I came back the next morning to enquire out of curiosity. By the way, **Le Petit Niçois** also offers the same *bouillabaisse* with *langoustes*. Its price: 168F.

I continued drinking the Gros Plant wine although I could also have had the local wine which traditionally goes with *bouillabaisse*: a *blanc* Cassis produced by the grower François Paret at Cassis near Marseille (108F a bottle and 62F for half a bottle). Another option from the extensive wine list was a Rosé de Provence in one of those characteristically shaped bottles which my table neighbours, a gaily conversing elderly Paris couple, were enjoying. Rosé de Provence is available at 58/36F, 72/45F, and 138F (AOC Bellet).

The atmosphere here at **Le Petit Niçois** is largely determined by the almost exclusively French clientèle who are quite obviously enjoying their meal and by the country décor: heavy, dark brown wooden beams above the service buffet (with wine goblets hanging from them), and along the whole ceiling. Old coach lamps in the back make for a thoroughly homely setting. A staircase leads to the impeccably clean toilets and also to a second dining room for another twenty or thirty guests.

While, in between eating and drinking, I was making some notes, the copious *bouillabaisse* slowly cooled down (and the white wine in the bottle became a little warmer), so that the *rouille* and the grated cheese did not melt as easily as before. But this did not spoil my enjoyment in the least.

Just before I finished eating, a small aluminium finger bowl with two slices of lemon in lukewarm water was brought to the table so that I could rinse my fingers before eating the *oeufs à la neige*. This dessert turned out to be a slab of poached meringue with a thin crust of caramel in a puddle of vanilla custard. At **Le Restaurant Bleu** (page 124) this dessert is freshly prepared, more attractive and also tastier, but then not everything is always perfect everywhere: *c'est la vie*!

After a cup of coffee (8F), I return home around eleven o'clock with a blissful feeling of complete satisfaction.

For less than 200F you can have a very agreeable evening here and enjoy a simple, honest, well prepared Provençal meal with accents from Nice.

Closed: *Monday midday and Sunday all day*
Métro: *8 La Tour Maubourg*   **Map:** *3*
Approximate price: *195F*
Fixed-price menu: *145F*

Aux Petits Oignons
20 rue de Bellechasse
Tel: 47.05.48.77

Between the Seine, near the Musée d'Orsay, and the boulevard Saint-Germain, there is a small bistro that is noteworthy not only for its décor and atmosphere but also for the special dishes that arrive in its quaint dining room from the little pink kitchen.

In these cosy surroundings I was welcomed one afternoon by a friendly young *garçon* clad in a white apron. On a small wooden buffet to the right of the entrance, dishes of fruit compote and trays of *pâtisserie* are on display and the house aperitif (a cherry wine) and other beverages are served from here, including the *"carafe d'eau municipale gratuite"*, the free pitcher of tap water advertised on a small board above the buffet. To the left, a long bench is flanked by nine small tables for two and vivid green chairs. A large still life of blue irises in a white vase is on the wall above. In the back, there are two more convivial tables for six. Pretty tablecloths and cotton napkins with a pattern of small flowers decorate the tables. From loudspeakers hidden behind small lamps agreeably soft classical music permeates the room.

The bill of fare lists ten cold and six hot entrées at prices between 24F and about 50F, including a fresh vegetable soup (*potage aux légumes* – 24F), a *salade mimosa* (lettuce with finely chopped hard-boiled eggs and *fines herbes* – 25F). Another hot entrée is the *anchoiade sur toasts* (toast spread with anchovy paste – 24F). Main dishes are the *plat du jour*, grilled chopped meat with pepper sauce, for instance, at 58F, *compôte de boeuf à la moutarde* at 64F, or *gigot d'agneau mijoté aux citrons confits* – leg of lamb simmered with preserved lemons at 74F. Desserts are 24F to 30F comprising such specialities as *mousse au chocolat "guanaja"* (referring to the origin of the cacao beans) and *cérises à l'eau-de-vie* (cherries in fruit brandy), while cheeses have such exotic names as *assiette de comté à la mendiante* (with nuts and other dried fruit) and *fromage grand père* (made of Roquefort, butter and Cognac), each costing 30F.

There is a very attractive three-course menu at 92F, served at lunch only, offering choices of four entrées, four main dishes and four desserts. Entrées include the fresh vegetable soup, chicken liver mousse, a cold purée of aubergine with olive oil, lemon juice, chopped garlic and onion (*caviar d'aubergine*) while main dishes can be *entrecôte de boeuf au grill* or roast chicken in a mustard crust. One of the desserts is a pudding with preserved apples and a caramel sauce.

It seemed a good choice to me to go for this moderately-priced menu and to abandon hunting for curiously named dishes on the intriguing bill of fare, keeping the price of the meal below the 200F mark.

So I had a *tourte aux trois viandes* as entrée, a light meat pie served hot with curly lettuce and tomato, well-prepared and tasty, although the meat content was certainly not over-generous. My main dish was braised chicken with a purée of carrots, broccoli, fine-grained rice and a light, tasty cream sauce. The portions were exactly right, neither too small nor too copious. The dessert was a *compôte aux trois parfums* consisting primarily of home-made apple stew with the addition of other flavours like pears. A half-litre carafe of the house red, a *vin de pays des Côtes-du-Tarn* from the south-west of France proved to be an appropriate companion for this simple, well-prepared meal.

I specially liked: the quaint, relaxed atmosphere, the imaginativeness of the bill of fare, and the set menu offering excellent value for money. The solitary eater, too, will easily feel at home here (which might not quite be the case in the new dining room on the first floor).

Open: *12 to 2 pm (12 to 1.30 pm on Saturday) and 8 to 11 pm*
Closed: *Sunday*
Métro: *12 Solférino*　　　　　　　　　　**Map:** *3*
Approximate price: *150F*
Fixed-price menu: *92F midday*

Au Petit Tonneau
20 rue Surcouf
Tel: 47.05.09.01

In 1977 Robert Courtine, the gastronomy editor of *Le Monde*, published a book with two hundred recipes from France's best female chefs. Not one of those recipes was taken from the repertoire of Ginette Boyer, cook-proprietress of **Au Petit Tonneau**, for two distinct reasons: Ginette did not take over this old bistro until 1979 and it was not Courtine but my good friend and mentor Jean-Pierre Imbach who discovered this *"cuisine de femme"* in 1980 and introduced it to the select audience of his original restaurant guide *Paris Gourmand*. Later on, in his *Géographie Gourmande de Paris (1983),* Courtine duly paid homage to Jean-Pierre Imbach for his discovery.

Near the entrance, on a broad buffet, a large, beautifully arranged bouquet of flowers catches the eye before disclosing a small display of some of the fresh produce to be transformed, refined and ennobled in the well-equipped miniature kitchen next to it. The floor is inlaid with small, irregularly shaped blue and brown mosaic tiles, the tables are covered with beige linen tablecloths and napkins, and here and there the walls are embellished with some frivolous and other less frivolous sketches on the subject of wine. On the bill of fare the regular dishes on offer are printed in black, while their prices are written by hand in brown ink, and under each heading there is some room to insert a few special dishes for the day such as fresh anchovies (35F), a fricassée of wild mushrooms (48F) or a *blanquette de lotte* (monk fish – 98F).

To begin with, I had a glass of cool, aromatic white Sauvignon for about 15F. The home-made *terrine de volaille* (poultry) at 42F is the most expensive of the thirteen entrées aside from the two salmon preparations (*en rillettes*, finely chopped and spiced – 58F, and smoked – 95F). The least expensive ones are the *cassolete de lentilles au lard* (hot lentils with bacon – 22F), the *crudités* at 25F and the cold salad of pork tongue at 28F.

I chose the terrine for which Madame Boyer is famous. Without inclining my head I could smell the enchanting scent emanating from it and I could discern small pieces of chicken liver in the coarse mass of the irregular pieces of pâté. And the taste? A poem of lightness and harmony, neither too dry nor too fatty, and a symphony of flavours. One more detail: the gherkins served with the terrine are not too acidic (as they can be all too often). I am already beginning to regret that I can't write a whole book about this old-fashioned, authentically fitted bistro which dates back to 1910, with its perfect bistro food, expertly and lovingly executed by tiny Ginette Boyer in her impeccably white cook's uniform. There would be more than enough aspects to be explored: Ginette belongs to the French association of women cooks, the *Association des Restauratrices-Cuisinières (ARC)* founded in 1975. Her bistro in the rue Surcouf has been awarded the rare *"Table de Maigret"* plaquette by the publishing house *Presses de la Cité* commemorating Georges Simenon, author of innumerable Maigret novels and, at the same time, authenticating the bistro *cuisine* so dear to Inspector Maigret. The inscription on the yellow brass plaque attached to a wall in the corner reads: *"Cette place est celle du Commissaire Principal Jules Maigret, hôte d'honneur gourmand de cette maison"*— "This place is reserved for Chief Inspector Jules Maigret, honorary guest-gourmand of this house". The meaning of the word *gourmand* is hard to convey since it implies quantity as well as quality; a *gourmand* is somebody who not only enjoys eating well, but heartily.

The *andouillette de Troyes dijonnaise* (55F), a perfect chitterling sausage in a light, delicate, frothy mustard-cream sauce, elicits the spontaneous remark from me that it is the sausage that "makes" the sauce and the sauce that "makes" the sausage. Rabelais, several hundred years ago, said something similar about the *andouille*, a dried, smoked and steamed pork tripe sausage which nowadays is eaten cold and thinly sliced as an *hors d'oeuvre*. He called mustard a *"beaume naturel et restaurant de l'andouille"*, a "natural balm and support of the andouille".

One of those real chitterling sausages, irregularly shaped, with an incomparable scent (you have to acquire the habit), and oh so delicately flavoured, sprinkled with fresh green herbs, what a treat! Everything is brought to the table glowing hot, the porcelain as well as the crisp, not-too-fatty French fried potatoes. But the *coeur de rumsteak saignant* (rare) *au roquefort* (65F) seems to please a solitary elderly gentleman who had come in shortly after me, equally well. Just like the *ris de veau frais* (fresh veal sweetbread) *braisé au porto* (95F) is obviously delighting a well-dressed young couple.

Fish is listed under *"suggestions du jour"* (the day's suggestions), for everything is fresh here, nothing comes out of tins or the freezer. Which reminds me of a recent newspaper cartoon, in which a guest remarks to a restaurant owner, "I thought that this was a three-star establishment?" and the restaurant owner answers sadly, "A common misunderstanding; it's the deep-freeze compartment of our refrigerator that has three stars".

I skipped the *plateau de fromages* (cheese board) which is 30F, in order to crown my meal with a piece of sizzling hot *tarte Tatin*, the famous caramelised apple tart, which is served with *crème fraîche* (slightly soured cream) here (38F), a small cup of coffee (10F) and a glass of old Armagnac (1974 – Château de Lacquy).

During my copious meal consisting of a series of high points of enjoyment in this thoroughly authentic bistro (where there are fresh flowers even in the toilet), a number of feelings and thoughts never before experienced to this degree of clarity emerged within me. Real tears of blissful enjoyment welled up in my eyes when confronted with yet another of the works of art from Ginette Boyer's kitchen, and while in the past I had sometimes thought that I ought to have been born earlier in order to have been able to enjoy some of the finer things of times gone by, here for the first time the thought crystallized in my mind that I would actually rather have been born a little later in order to be able to come here, to Ginette Boyer's **Petit Tonneau**, all the more often.

In the meantime, I have been here several times with or without company, but always to my heart's content. And I have noticed that, although there are more and more people finding their way here, a ninety-five-year-old gentleman from Reims also still comes here regularly to relish the kind of food that reminds him so intensely of his grandmother's cooking.

Closed: *Sunday*
Métro: *8, 13, RERB Invalides or 8 La Tour Manbourg* **Map: 3**
Approximate price: *210F*

Au Pied de Fouet
45 rue de Babylone
Tel: 47 05 12 27

With room for just sixteen people, this is probably one of the smallest restaurants in Paris. Located on a rather sombre street, just around the corner from the rue de Vaneau, **Au Pied de Fouet** features a modest but authentic *zinc* (the traditional tin-covered bar of an authentic old bistro) to the left of the doorway, where an aperitif can be enjoyed before and a cup of coffee after your meal. This releases pressure on the banquette along the wall and the three tables and six chairs in front. At the back of the room, underneath a wide fitment with fifty-six small pigeonholes for personal table napkins of the regulars, there is another small table for four. That, and the pocket-handkerchief-sized kitchen, is all. That is, if you don't count "upstairs", a floor suspended from high above the dining area and not in use at present. The *patronne* proudly informed me that this architectural curiosity inspired Le Corbusier around 1919 to design his famous *maison à toit-jardin* (house with roof terrace).

The customers are almost all regulars, but no one is made to feel a stranger — the *patron* behind the *zinc* has a friendly word and smile for everyone.

One look at the bill of fare reveals an ample choice of entrées at around 10F such as *taboulé* (a refreshing salad of semolina soaked in the juice of sliced cucumber and diced tomatoes and dressed with chopped onions, mint and parsley, lots of lemon juice and some olive oil, a preparation of Lebanese origin), a salad of noodles, celeriac and carrots or of chicory, potatoes and hard-boiled eggs, *rillette de la Sarthe* (finely chopped pork slowly simmered for a long time in its own fat), hard-boiled eggs with mayonnaise . . .

Main courses (42F to 55F) vary from fillet of plaice in breadcrumbs (*carrelet*) and fillet of salmon in an excellent chive sauce (*à la ciboulette*) to *tripes à la provençale* and flank of beef (*onglet*) with mashed potatoes. After cheese (Saint-Nectaire, Brie – 10F) there is a wide variety of desserts available at the same modest prices as the *hors d'oeuvre:* pies, tarts, pastries (apples, cherries), almonds, *génoises* . . .), dried prunes in red wine, *clafoutis* (batter cake with fruit), etcetera.

I opted for a cream of vegetable soup followed by hot tongue with watercress sauce and steamed potatoes (*langue de boeuf au cresson et pommes vapeur*). Everything, the tongue, the vegetable sauce and the garnishing, was abundant, lovingly prepared and carefully presented. I was very much taken by the potatoes which had a distinct flavour of their own, reminding me of the importance of being just as meticulous in the choice of this humble vegetable as when sampling more expensive fish or meat.

For dessert, I tried the *oeufs à la neige au caramel,* small clouds of meringue served floating on vanilla custard. **Au Pied de Fouet**'s version of this classic *entremet* was at least equal in flavour and quantity to the same dish I had eaten a few days before in a very good restaurant at twice the price.

My meal was accompanied by a half bottle of young Gamay de Touraine from the vineyards of Henri Marionnet at Soings for 26.50F (53F the bottle). There is also an excellent Anjou–Villages Clos de Médicin for 65F (32.50F half). The most expensive wine on the list is a red Graves for 70F. The house red and white wines are priced at 20F a carafe of 45 cl (10F for 23 cl). Try the refreshing, spicy Sauvignon de Touraine from the same grower as the Gamay (53F a bottle and 26.50F a half bottle).

While finishing a cup of coffee (4F) at *le zinc*, I noticed a poem framed on a wall, an ode to **Au Pied de Fouet**, which Andrée, the friendly *patronne*, told me had been written a few years ago by a regular customer. To my mind, it very vividly and accurately sums up the daily routine and atmosphere of this and many other little bistros described in this guidebook.

Open: 12 - 2 pm; 7 - 9 pm
Closed: *Saturday evening; Sunday*
Métro: 10 Vaneau or 13 Saint-François-Xavier or 10, 12 Sèvres
Babylone   *Map: 3*
Approximate price: 115F

Babet, le 19 novembre 1983
A Andrée, Martial et Christine

Petite porte discrète et fermée,
Fenêtre assombrie par un voile de carreaux.

La porte s'ouvre:
Un flot de paroles assaille l'arrivant.
Le Pied de Fouet déborde du monde
Ce sont essentiellement des habitués
Le midi, ce sont les bureaux qui se précipitent chez Andrée.
Par contre, le soir, on a plus de chance d'être tranquille.

Au milieu de tous ces gens,
Martial, derrière son bar, impassible,
Toujours une bouteille à la main,
Observe les clients et fait les additions.
Soudain dans tout ce tumulte,
Apparaît une petite tête avec des plats plein les mains.
C'est Andrée, remarquable par le son de sa voix.
Elle dirige, gronde, place les gens
D'une manière decidée et efficace.
Souvent les nouveaux, un peu bousculés, prennent la mouche
Et les habitués sourient de bon coeur.
Mais Andrée a la répartie vive
Et tout rentre dans l'ordre.

Au fond, on voit de temps en temps
La tête de Dédé apparaître
Et échanger deux, trois mots avec un client.
Puis Mamid sort de la cuisine
Pour ramener des réserves de nourriture.
Et apporter de l'eau chaude à Martial au comptoir.
Parfois une silhouette silencieuse et menue, Christine,
Se faufile et salue les connaissances.

Comme on se sent bien - Dans l'ambiance familiale
du Pied de Fouet!

To: Andrée, Martial and Christine

Small door, hidden and closed
Windows veiled by check curtains.

The door swings open:
A wave of chatter engulfs the newcomer.
The Pied de Fouet overflows with people,
Regulars to a man or woman.
At midday it's the office workers who pour into Andrée's.
But at dinner you have more of a chance of a quiet evening.

Amidst all those people,
Martial impassive behind his bar,
With a bottle always at hand,
Watches over the guests and keeps track of their bills.
Suddenly, from all this hubbub,
A small head emerges and hands full of dishes.
It's Andrée, known immediately by the sound of her voice.
She directs people, tells them off, and seats them
Resolutely and efficiently.
Often the uninitiated, a bit perturbed, will take offence,
But the regulars will smile good-naturedly.
Andrée dispenses witty repartee
And everything settles down.

In the back, from time to time,
Dédé's head will emerge
To exchange a word or two with a client.
Then it's Mamid, coming from the kitchen,
To replenish the food.
And furnish hot water to Martial behind his counter.
Once in a while, a silent and fragile silhouette, Christine,
Looms up, greeting some acquaintances.

Oh, how happy one feels — In the homely welcome
of the Pied de Fouet!

Gare du Nord, Opéra

Arrondissements 8, 9 and 10

Le Relais Beaujolais
3 rue Milton
Tel: 48.78.77.91

It was Alain Mazeau who, in 1985, from behind the counter of **Ma Bourgogne** on the boulevard Haussmann (see page 155) expertly helped to arrange my wine exploration from Pouilly-sur-Loire to Chablis and on to Juliénas in the Beaujolais region and finally to Haut-Poitou, an old wine district between the river deltas of the Loire and the Gironde. A *voyage vineuse* whose route had derived from **Ma Bourgogne**'s bottles and glasses and passed into my bloodstream and finally my memory.

On a recent visit I failed to find Alain at his old place; in April 1987, after working at **Ma Bourgogne** for twenty years, he took over **Le Relais Beaujolais** on the corner of the rue Milton and the rue Hippolyte-Lebas, an old-fashioned bistro where the wood-covered *zinc* has not been debased to the function of a mere service counter and where ten or twelve carefully set tables decorated with lovingly arranged flowers invite his guests each midday and evening to enjoy generous, well-prepared food at reasonable prices.

Since this is the only place I know in Paris which so happily combines classical bistro-restaurant and wine bistro, I seized the chance of spending a little time at the lively *zinc* to try some of the wines on offer by the glass before settling down in the cosy dining room close by.

You can rely upon Alain Mazeau always to have an excellent white Mâcon in store such as the incomparable Mâcon-Bussières 1985 which I was privileged to taste in 1988, and most recently the 1987 Mâcon-Clessé of the Domaine René Michel et ses Fils which showed a lot of character and backbone, priced at 9.50F per glass. The 1988 Mâcon-Villages at 7F a glass was less expressive but more acidic and had less character than the Clessé. Also available was a red Saumur-Champigny for 8F a glass and a 1986 Chinon at

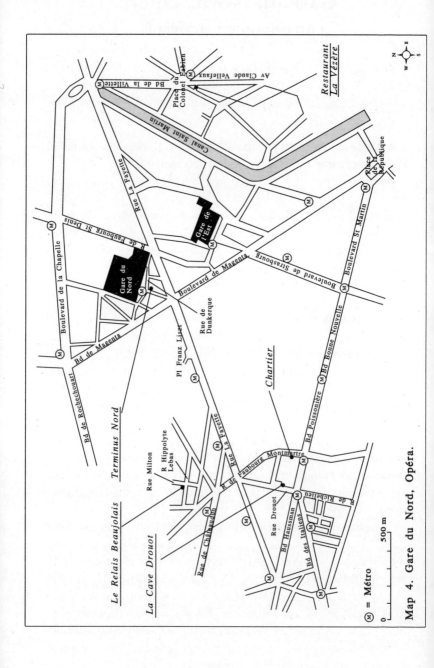

Map 4. Gare du Nord, Opéra.

Ⓜ = Métro

0   500 m

8.50F. And a whole gamut of Beaujolais growths: Brouilly, Chénas, Chiroubles, Juliénas, Saint-Amour, Moulin-à-Vent, Regnié, are available at between 8.50F and 11.50F a glass, befitting the name of this bistro. With such a seductive choice on hand, no wonder you will not smell a pungent glass of *pastis* (Pernod etcetera) at **Le Relais Beaujolais'** *zinc.* There is, however, an *apéritif maison*, jokingly called "*truc maison*" by regulars, a mixture of tiny amounts of *cassis* (blackcurrant) and *framboise* (raspberry) liqueurs and cool red Beaujolais (a variation on the *kir* theme) priced at 9.50F at the *zinc* and 16.50F served on a pretty silver tray at a table by Marie-Christine, Alain's charming wife. It is then accompanied by butter and a small earthenware pot of *rillettes* (a creamy paste of minced pork long and deliciously simmered) that can be spread on the well-flavoured white bread that is automatically brought to each table.

The bill of fare is equally up to expectations aroused by a Relais Beaujolais: *salade beaujolaise, rosette de Beaujolais* (dry pork sausage), *jambon persillé* (ham in parsleyed white wine jelly), *oeufs en meurette* (poached eggs in a red wine sauce), *saucisson chaud pommes à l'huile* (hot pork sausage with potato salad) are all typical regional dishes. These are priced at between 35F and 58F. But you can also make do with a very generously and carefully arranged *assiette de crudités* (raw vegetables) for 30F or a simple *museau vinaigrette* (salad of ox muzzle) for 35F.

I was pleasantly surprised by my salad of *pissenlits au lard* (tender dandelion leaves with bacon − 45F) which had been expertly tossed by the *patron* on the central service table and is (optionally) served with a warm poached egg which pleasantly enhanced the flavour and texture of the salad.

From the 130F three-course menu (including a cup of coffee) which is served only at midday, I had the *onglet de veau à l'échalote* (flank of veal with shallots), three small slices of tender, juicy and well-flavoured meat with an excellent shallot sauce and perfectly crisp French fried potatoes plus a tall earthenware pot of gherkins with wooden pincers to one side.

A bottle of 1988 Beaujolais-Villages from the Cave Bel Air at Saint-Jean-d'Ardières (75F) is set down on the table by a waiter clad in black apron, white shirt and black bow tie. You only need pay for what you drink, but it is so light, fresh and delicious that I had finished it before the dessert, *tarte Tatin*, caramelized apple pie, came to my table and provided a final satisfaction before I finished with a steaming cup of coffee.

The dining room is decorated in country style with heavy wooden beams, wood panelling along the walls, stuffed game birds, a small antique wine press and wrought iron lamps. The tables are covered with yellow embroidered tablecloths, there are generous white linen napkins and beautifully sparkling wine glasses. At about twelve thirty people start moving from the *zinc* into the dining room.

Some more items from the bill of fare that I have noted: a beautiful *salade de crustacés et langouste aux fines herbes* for 150F which is not only a feast for the eye, but quite obviously for palate and humour too, as is borne out by two young ladies in animated conversation at the counter savouring this dish together with a glass of Beaujolais. Another regular item on the menu is preserved duck with sautéed potatoes for 78F, also the calf's kidneys with *moutarde de Meaux* for 125F, a slice of leg of lamb, pot-roasted with tomatoes and garlic *(provençale)*. And of course there are snails, served in small porcelain vessels instead of in their own fragile shells. The special dishes of the day on my most recent visit were fillet of monkfish with fennel (115F) and *médaillon de veau à la crème* (veal – 125F). The cheese board priced at 35F is optional with the 130F fixed-price menu instead of a dessert. Desserts include *mousse au chocolat, crème caramel, île flottante* (soft meringue, caramelized and served on a vanilla custard) and are on offer for 30F.

Generosity, style and quality are three of the main characteristics of this well-established wine restaurant in a quiet and picturesque part of the ninth *arrondissement*. Don't forget to reserve if you want to eat here. The *zinc* is reserved for dinner guests after nine in the evening, but at any other hour you can always pop in for a glass of wine.

Open: *from 9 am*
Closed: *Saturday & Sunday*
Métro: *12 Notre-Dame-de-Lorette*   **Map:** *4*
Approximate price: *210F*

Chartier
7 rue Faubourg-Montmartre
Tel: 47.70.86.29

A dining room the size of a large railway station, in the style of the turn of the century: a stately, high ceiling, lots of mirrors and enormous chandeliers . . . you are at **Chartier** amidst a bustling crowd of all sorts and sizes, who have come here to have a wholesome meal for very little money, or just to admire the surroundings and enjoy the atmosphere while nibbling away at something simple. They are served quickly and efficiently by a small army of experienced waiters in classical outfits (black waistcoat and tie, white apron).

The bill of fare, which is typed afresh each day, offers a wide choice of various entrées, main dishes and desserts. Soup 6F, various salads 9F, pâté, sausage, brawn (*museau*), ham 9F to 16F, meat and fish dishes 25F to 40F, cheeses 6F to 9F, pastries, fruit, *mousse au chocolat*, etcetera, 8F to 15F, ice cream 9F to 17F. Side dishes of vegetables including French fried potatoes and pasta are available for 7F or 8F, while butter, mayonnaise, gherkin and the like can be ordered for 1.50F. Bread and water of course are free with your meal as in any French restaurant.

The most expensive dish on the bill of fare is a dozen snails for 46F, listed as an entrée.

You have a very limited budget? Try the pink shrimps with butter (*crevettes roses* – 16F), followed by roast leg of lamb (*gigot* – 37F), or begin with a hard-boiled egg with mayonnaise (8F), that most classical of all classical bistro entrées, and continue with a dish of lamb's brains with parsley butter (*cervelle d'agneau maître d'hôtel*) for 28F, garnished with green peas (*petits pois*) for an extra 8F. A piece of Camembert (6F), a 25cl carafe of the very drinkable house red wine (7F) and a cup of coffee (5F) will adequately complete this meal for the thrifty visitor. If you are not very hungry you can make do with some cold ham with gherkin for 9F, accompanied by sautéed cauliflower (8F) or a portion of Alsatian sauerkraut (*choucroute* – 7F), some goat's cheese (9F) and a quarter of a litre of red house wine or a small bottle of beer or cider for 8 or 9F plus coffee, and your bill will still be under 40F.

I started out with the *museau de boeuf vinaigrette* (13F) and continued with a veal *escalope* with green peas (40F plus 8F). With it, I had a half bottle of red Corbières wine for 15F. Together with an espresso coffee this quick meal came to about 80F.

Chartier offers honest, unpretentious cooking. The service is friendly, matter-of-fact and prompt. The hard-working waiters who, like circus performers, balance up to a dozen plates in the narrow aisles between the tables amidst the steady ebb and flow of visitors, are a sight worth watching.

There is another **Chartier** restaurant, **Le Drouot** at 103 rue Richelieu in the 2nd arrondissement with a first-floor dining room. But I strongly recommend sampling the atmosphere of the old **"bouillon Chartier"** at the upper end of the rue Faubourg-Montmartre in a small alleyway across the street from the old *Palace* theatre. (This, by the way, now houses a large, trendy night club where you can easily pay over a thousand francs for a bottle of Champagne.)

I specially appreciated: **Chartier**'s late nineteenth century décor, its bustling atmosphere, and the great variety of simple, well-prepared dishes at modest prices. What a difference compared to the equally traditional but much more sedate and more expensive establishment **Le Train Bleu** (see page 113)! The two historic restaurants differing so widely in style and atmosphere, your own personal taste, the particular mood you happen to be in and the budget at your disposal will best help you make up your mind which one to visit. Why not try both if you have the time?

Open: *Seven days a week from 11 am to 3 pm and from 6 to 9.30 pm*
Métro: *RueMontmartre 8, 9*   **Map:** *4*
Approximate price: *75F*
No reservations

La Cave Drouot
8 rue Drouot
Tel: 47.70.83.38

A few steps from **Au Duc de Richelieu,** just across the boulevard Montmartre, surrounded by stamp collectors' shops and auctioneers *(commissaires priseurs)* with their characteristic oval signboards, on the corner of the rue Rossini, you will find Jean-Pierre Cachau's **Cave Drouot.** A pigeonloft? A beehive? The perpetual coming and going of all kinds of visitors who drop in to have a quick glass of wine, a *panaché* (a mixture of beer and lemonade, like a shandy) or a small cup of coffee at the gleaming brass-covered *zinc* evokes this kind of comparison. The way in which most newcomers are amicably greeted by the hard-working waiters (clad in black aprons, white shirts and black bow ties) shows that they are old friends of the house. But the stranger also receives a warm welcome as I experienced when I came in on a Monday afternoon around three-thirty to sample a glass of dark red Madiran wine (8.50F for 8cl) and eat a few slices of wholesome Poilâne sourdough bread with cured, air-dried Bayonne ham (22F for four large slices).

The last guests in the adjacent dining room were in the process of a cordial and extensive goodbye with the generous *patron* Jean-Pierre Cachau and his charming blonde wife Mado. The company had obviously enjoyed a lavish meal centring on one of the three *plats du jour,* which change daily according to what is best available at the market. (No fish on Monday, nothing is landed over the weekend, and no offal either – there is no slaughtering on Saturday and Sunday.)

On one visit, a terrine of rabbit in a cucumber cream sauce was available as entrée (about 50F), as well as *confit de canard maison* (a speciality from south-western France: preserved duck). Fillet of beef with oyster mushrooms and roast rack of lamb with a green mustard sauce were on offer as main dishes for about 90F each. On another occasion the three main dishes of the day were: *blanquette de veau* (creamy veal stew – 70F), *poulet fermier rôti à la moutarde* (farmhouse chicken –75F), and *gigot d'agneau à la crème de thym* (leg of lamb – 82F).

The extensive bill of fare features such standard entrées as *cervelas vinaigrette, rillettes, saucisson sec,* etcetera, for about 35F, *jambon de Bayonne* or *jambon à l'os* (raw cured and air-dried ham or cooked ham cut from the bone) for a few francs more, and marinated anchovy with warm potato salad. The excellent *pâté basque* is 35F.

Besides the abundantly served *plats du jour,* basic roasts are available too, such as *côte de boeuf* (rib of beef − 87F), *faux filet* (sirloin − 68F), and *bavette* (literally: bib, the specifically French cut of skirt of beef − 59F).

Cheeses, too, are very good here and a small selection costs about 36F. Various home-made pastries are available at prices depending on their composition, the bill of fare tells us.

Naturally, an extensive wine list offers prestigious growths from the Bordeaux and Rhône regions as well as from Burgundy; and the outstanding Châteauneuf-du-Pape made by grower Paul Avril at the Domaine du Clos des Papes.

You can have your midday meal in the rather crowded but comfortable dining room reached through a passage from the bar, or on the more quiet glassed-in terrace (called *brasserie* here) looking out on the rue Rossini; or in the separate first-floor dining room at one of the sixteen or seventeen small tables which are usually taken by twelve-thirty.

Back to the *zinc* where the wines that have been tasted, selected, bought and bottled by the *patron* are available by the glass. Juliénas, Chénas, Morgon, Fleurie, and above all a really excellent Côte-de-Brouilly (from the grower Robert Verger at Saint-Lager) form an impressive phalanx of Beaujolais growths and are sold for around 8F a glass of 8cl. A simple white Cheverny from the Loire valley a few kilometres south-west of Orléans, made from the Sauvignon grape, costs only 4.50F. A refreshing Quincy from a small wine growing district on the river Cher, about a hundred kilometres south of Orléans, also made from the Sauvignon grape, is available at 7.50F, the same as an excellent white Mâcon. A very special, golden yellow, mellow Pacherenc-du-Vic-Bilh (produced by Beheity at Aydie), on offer for 8.50F, originates from south-western France, just like the Madiran (domaine Damiens), the *jambon de Bayonne* and . . . the *patron.*

Other more solid options from which to choose while sampling these wines: *rillettes,* cheeses (25F), *pâté basque* (very good!), and an *assiette de charcuterie* (37F); the same with various hams costs 46F.

What I especially appreciated here, besides the excellent quality of the food and the wine is the sympathetic friendliness of the waitresses in the dining areas and the waiters behind the bar, all alert and attentive even when extremely pressed for time. The framed *Diplôme de la Courtoisie Française* which adorns the wall opposite the *zinc* is certainly deserved.

Open: *7.30 am to 9.00 pm*
Closed: *Sunday*
Métro: *8, 9 Richelieu Drouot*   **Map:** *4*
Approximate price: *230F*

Terminus Nord
23 rue du Dunkerque
Tel: 42.85.05.15

This was a new eating experience for me in a "modern" chain of restaurants in Paris. **Terminus Nord** is rather a *brasserie*, with its display of shellfish and crustaceans on the pavement, its continuous service from 11 am to 12.30 am, and its regular choucroute specialities, although there is not the usual *brasserie* emphasis on beer. It is located right across the street from the main entrance of the Gare du Nord in the centre of Paris. The trains operating from this railway station serve the north of France and, of course, its northern neighbours Belgium, the Netherlands and Britain. **Terminus Nord** is one of a chain of restaurants which have the same style of décor, service, *cuisine,* and prices.

A fixed-price menu, consisting of *hareng de la Baltique à la crème, choucroute spéciale, sorbet au choix,* a quarter of a litre of *vin blanc d'Alsace*, and coffee can be had for 137F while these items, taken *à la carte*, would come to 183F. Of course, you might then get larger portions in some instances, and you would have the choice. This is the way a lot of Parisian restaurants work. Others, like **Chartier** (p.87), to save people the worry of choosing, offer a menu suggestion for a price that is exactly the sum total of the component dishes. **Terminus Nord** does not seem to be over-anxious to sell their low-price menu because it is set out in small letters at the bottom of the bill of fare simply as *"menu promotionnel"* without any indication of its scope. The waiter, however, was very helpful when I asked him to explain the details of this special offer.

Aside from several *choucroute* dishes between 68F and 92F, there are about seven fish dishes from fried whiting arranged tail in mouth (*merlan en colère*) for 67F, via cod (*cabillaud*, 78F) to *sole meunière* (104F). The choice of meat dishes offered includes such basics as *fricassée de volaille* (chicken stew, 92F), *entrecôte beurre maître d'hôtel* (95F), and a slice of leg of lamb (*tranche de gigot*) grilled with garlic for 93F. Oysters of various sorts and sizes and other shellfish and crustaceans are listed on a separate menu (oysters from 54F to 129F for half a dozen, Spanish mussels at 60F a dozen, fresh crab with mayonnaise for 89.50F). The most attractive is, of course, the *plateau de fruits de mer* for 176F which excels in its abundance and above all in its extreme freshness, the most essential quality with all sea food, and guaranteed by the immense turnover of **Terminus Nord**. All shellfish here are served with the customary rye bread, butter, lemon, and vinegar with shallots.

I resisted the temptation of this special attraction when visiting **Terminus Nord** on a Sunday afternoon in March, and was promptly rewarded with a surprisingly large bowl of fresh *crevettes grises* (unshelled shrimps) served as a complimentary side dish with the glass of cool, refreshing Riesling that I had ordered as an aperitif. Riesling by the glass was not marked on the wine list and was billed at the price of the *kir au pinot d'Alsace*: 17.50F. Quite a bargain – if you manage to keep the bowl of shrimps long enough to enjoy more than two or three of these delicious little sea creatures before one of the extremely efficient waiters takes it away when you are not looking.

I started off my meal with a simple tomato salad garnished with coarse onion rings and lettuce and sprinkled with chives (22F, the cheapest *hors d'oeuvre*, the most expensive being the *salade riche au foie gras* at 79.50F) and continued with the *choucroute spécial* (82F), a surprisingly small dish of mild, crisply cooked *choucroute* garnished with lots of juniper berries, two types of sausage, one thick and one thin, a slice of cooked salt pork, one of smoked pork and a boiled potato. The *jarret fumé sur choucroute* (smoked pork knuckle) for 68F seems more copious and may well be a better choice for the really hungry. An earthenware pot of hot mustard with a small wooden spoon is served with the *choucroute* as vinegar and oil had been with the tomato salad. The half-litre carafe of Sylvaner, a simple, refreshing white Alsace wine (39F) is brought in a small metal bucket of ice water – a welcome gesture: this way, even carafe wine is kept cool during the meal. My wine glass is filled whenever empty or nearly empty by one of the many young waiters and waitresses taking coats and suitcases to and from the basement.

Between the many green plants and *étagères* placed in a seemingly haphazard fashion throughout the spacious dining room, making for lots of cosy corners instead of leaving a vast open array of tables, I can see that the clientèle is composed of a mixture of elderly French people, out for a typical Sunday lunch, young couples enjoying aperitifs and gigantic two-storey platters of seafood with Sancerre (143F a bottle, 78F a half bottle), as well as tourists and travellers of various nationalities taking advantage of the convenient baggage storage in the basement while enjoying their meals.

The *délices du maître fromager* (39.50F) are presented on an abundant cheese board with a little paper flag on each cheese giving the name of the . . . cheese merchant. I selected a Brie de Meaux which turned out a bit gluey, a spicy and very tasty Valançay, a pyramid shaped goat's cheese from the Touraine, a Munster, a cheese from eastern France which promised a pungent flavour, but was unfortunately a bit too young to fully reveal it, a Roquefort which was predominantly salty, and a very fine goat's cheese of the Crottin de Chavignol type. From the wine list I chose a half bottle of red Gamay de Touraine 1989 (41F; 75.50F for a whole bottle) from the good wine grower Henry Marionnet, which turned out to be fruity and full-bodied, was served at the right, cool temperature and proved a perfect companion for the cheeses.

I concluded my leisurely meal with a *tarte aux pommes campagnardes*, a country apple tart with currants and raisins, served warm with a generous bowl of slightly sour cream (*crème fraîche*) for

33F, one of the eighteen desserts from the separate *gourmandises* list (27.50F, *crème caramel*; 49.50F *crêpes flambées à Grand Marnier*). The ensuing coffee at 12.50F, served in a somewhat elaborate manner, was a cup of steaming hot espresso which was by no means too strong.

Presentation and service at **Terminus Nord** are excellent if sometimes a little too fast. The relation between the service and the quality of the dishes, however, is somewhat out of balance. *"Hygiénique et économique"*, the words on an electric hot air hand-dryer in the basement men's room two flights of stairs down, adequately summarised the total impression **Terminus Nord** made on me.

Open: *11 am to 12.30 am, 7 days a week*
Métro: *4, 5 RER B, Gare du Nord*   **Map:** *4*
Approximate price: *260F*
Fixed-price menu: *137F*

Restaurant La Vézère
37 avenue Claude-Vellefaux
Tel: 42.05.30.01

A faithful reader of the first edition of this guidebook furnished this address in the tenth *arrondissement*, a central district of Paris where good restaurants are more difficult to find than elsewhere in the city. It is one of the few Parisian restaurants which, without joining the price-inflating cult of truffles and *foie gras*, specialises in the authentic regional *cuisine* of the Périgord which is counted among the best in France. For Curnonsky (1872–1956), the famous *chroniqueur gastronomique avant la lettre*, elected Prince-Gastronome by restaurant chefs in a referendum held in 1927, butter was indispensable to good cooking. And yet, for the *cuisine périgourdine*, he coined the famous epithet of a *"cuisine sans beurre et sans reproche"*, cooking without butter and without reproach.

In Périgord, fattening geese is a widespread practice with a long tradition. Truffles also are collected there in appreciable quantities. But high-priced items such as fattened goose liver (*foie gras d'oie*) or those black subterranean mushrooms that are called truffles, are not to be found on **La Vézère**'s small bill of fare, handwritten by the *patronne* with a coarse black felt-tip pen. There is, however, a portion of fresh duck liver available at 75F. But apart from that, the prices are as small as the dining room with its two round tables for four and eight square tables for two. Luckily, the same does not go for the portions, witness the *confit de canard pommes sarladaises* for 85F. Set down before me on an oval plate this consisted of a substantial leg and thigh of duck which had been shallow-fried after having been cooked and preserved in duck fat. Duck fat also had been used in baking the sliced potato served as accompaniment. Instead of being sprinkled with a mixture of finely chopped garlic and parsley (as the classic recipe prescribes), the *pommes sarladaises* had been garnished with a branch of fresh curly parsley, a slice of peeled tomato covered with a tasty mousse of garlic and parsley and several slices of courgette encrusted with browned, melted cheese.

The cooking is good here and the dishes are inventively and lovingly prepared and copiously served by the young *patron* in the kitchen. Quite a treat!

Other dishes on the bill of fare: *cassoulet au confit de canard* (a casserole containing white haricot beans and preserved duck – 90F), *escalope périgourdine* (a thin slice of meat with Armagnac – 82F) and some grilled cuts of beef for between 72F and 85F. Remarkable also a *coq au vin de Cahors* for 88F (chicken stewed in red Cahors wine with onions, bacon and button mushrooms).

Entrées include crab cocktail (49F) and salad with bacon (49F). A simple *salade de saison* is available at 25F. But you can also start with a salad of smoked breast of duck *(maigret de canard fumé)* for 58F.

It is mostly regulars from the offices in the vicinity who come to eat here at midday and who go back to work afterwards. This may be one of the reasons why wine is not the most cherished item in this small, quiet eating place. The simple house Cahors for 75F has an agreeably fruity scent of blackberries and a rather neutral flavour which harmonises with almost anything, even weith the tasty *tarte des demoiselles Tatin* (38F), that famous upside-down caramelised apple tart named after the baker's daughters in the village of Lamotte-Beuvron south of Orléans where this pastry was "invented" generations ago by a girl working in their bakery.

The *vacherin (framboises ou noisettes)* which also adorns the list of desserts is not cheese as its name might suggest, but a meringue filled with ice cream, fruit and whipped cream. Its form and colour vividly recall the alpine cheese of the same name. There is a cheese board, too, of course (38F).

Lots of large, beautiful photographs and paintings from the Vézère region, part of the Dordogne province, decorate the walls of this quiet, authentic regional neighbourhood restaurant in that somewhat gloomy part of the tenth *arrondissement*.

Open: *12 to 2.00 pm*
Closed: *Evenings and all day Saturday and Sunday*
Métro: *2, Colonel-Fabien, exit Claude-Vellefaux* **Map:** *4*
Approximate price: *180F*

Beaubourg, Marais, Bastille, Gare de Lyon

Arrondissements 4, 11 and 12

Restaurant Antoine (Chez Marcel)
7 rue Saint-Nicolas
Tel: *43.43.49.40*

In a small, somewhat dusky and quiet side street off the busy rue du Faubourg-Saint-Antoine, crowded with the furniture stores and workshops typical of this neighbourhood, there is, hidden behind an unobtrusive façade, a restaurant of very distinct charm.

When I arrived for a third visit on a sunny Thursday, a little after one o'clock, I felt reassured on entering, seeing all these tables set and ready — somewhat like a Prodigal Son returning home, as if all this had been arranged to please me and make me feel comfortable — and in a way, it had.

I had booked a table to make sure, and the *patronne* greeted me with a friendly smile before escorting me to a large table (for four) covered with solid beige linen. Immediately afterwards, a young waitress put down three bottles next to the large balloon wine glasses that were already on the table: a Muscadet de Sèvre-et-Maine *sur lie* (domaine de l'Alouette, Jacques Barré, *viticulteur* at Mouzillon-Vallet, in one of the best regions of the *appellation*), a bottle of Crème de Cassis de Bourgogne (blackcurrant liqueur) produced by Védrenne père et fils at Nuits-Saint-Georges, and a Beaujolais-Villages. That is the custom here. So you can decide for yourself how much *crème de cassis* you want in your *kir* or you can simply have a glass of cool white, very lightly sparkling Muscadet as aperitif. (*Sur lie* means that the wine has been left after fermentation on its lees and bottled directly without filtering the following spring.) On your bill you will be charged only for what you actually drank (on the basis of 70F for the bottle of Muscadet, 80F for the Beaujolais and nothing for the *crème de cassis*). Of course, you can also make a *kir* with red wine

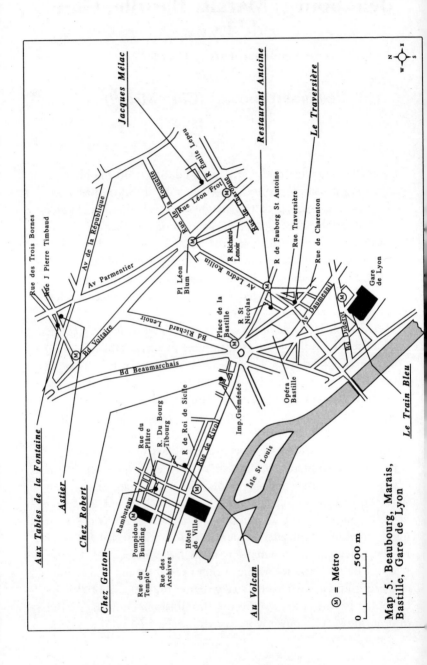

Map 5. Beaubourg, Marais, Bastille, Gare de Lyon

Ⓜ = Métro

0   500 m

like the two gentlemen who have just taken their seats at the table facing mine.

There is a fixed-price menu for 145F including a choice of three entrées: chicken liver terrine, vegetable terrine with a mousse of *foie gras*, or avocado with octopus; two main courses: chitterling sausage or roast saddle of lamb, both with sauté potatoes; and cheese or honey and walnut ice cream. This menu also includes a cup coffee in conclusion.

The bill of fare offers a wide choice of interesting entrées: terrines (duck with walnuts, rabbit with prunes, young wild boar (*marcassin*) from 52F to 55F, sausages including two different *andouilles* (wafer-thin slices of smoked pork tripe sausage) for 65F, *rillettes à l'oie* (potted minced pork with goose) and brawn, 50F each. And the show piece of the place: *les cochonnailles assorties* for 98F per person. This is a whole spread: five or six large sausages, lots of terrines, bowls with salad of lentils, radishes . . . a feast, especially when ordered for a party of three or four. It is admittedly not cheap and it will be charged "*obligatoirement*" for each guest, as is especially mentioned on the menu to preclude any misunderstandings. But you can eat as much as you want of everything there – and that is what makes it so interesting: to be able to sample all these different sausages and terrines one after the other, during one course. Naturally it may be difficult to leave enough room for anything afterwards! There are less expensive entrées too: salads for between 30F and 45F, snails for 46F or 52F, the latter being twelve *petits gris*, small, especially delicate ones, while you get six "normal" ones for 46F.

Several cold fish dishes cost between 50F and 96F.

I ordered a lentil salad (30F) and a huge earthenware tureen of lentils with baby onions, sliced onions and herbs and a generous bowl of good home-made vinaigrette were brought to my table; again the idea is that you take as much as you want.

My main dish was a *saucisson chaud,* a whole hot pork sausage with green peppercorns and potato salad. What an explosion of flavours! This is probably the best *saucisson chaud* I have ever eaten. And the potato salad is appetisingly garnished with fresh green herbs and thinly cut onion rings and seasoned with delicious vegetable oil.

It seems unbelievable that there is still room for about twenty people at a quarter to two and it strikes me suddenly that these twenty "missing people" are probably, at this very moment, being chased through a microwave meal by some overworked waiter in one of those showy establishments that adorn the *grands boulevards*.

The people who have the good fortune to be here are carrying on lively conversations, the very best background music there can be. The pleasure and happiness their faces radiate is reflected in my own feelings and the Beaujolais I am drinking with my meal is not only "artfully chosen" as the label rather pretentiously proclaims, but drinking it really is a pleasure as the same label predicts.

Other interesting items on the bill of fare: *andouillette* (76F), pig's trotters (85F), *onglet* (flank of beef – 96F). The *patronne* will tell you what the day's special dishes are when presenting the bill of fare: *boeuf bourguignon, tripes maison* or *coq au vin*. I had the latter here once, and it was a portion that would have fed three hungry miners. The cheese platter is 45F and desserts are available for between 42F and 50F. Sorbets cost 45F. If you order the fresh pineapple dessert (45F) here, you will not get a plate with a few slices of pineapple on it, but a gigantic goblet full of chunks of fresh fruit, decorated with a cap of pineapple rind with leaves. Again, you take as much as you want – you are in a house of plenty here.

I relived another one of those precious moments in this authentic bistro when the *poires au vin* (42F) were brought to my table: whole pears with lots of red wine sauce in a large porcelain bowl – a successful marriage of flavours.

Quite a few business people from the neighbourhood come to eat here, and that is usually their only complete meal that day, as the *patronne* told me (not to my surprise). This is decidedly not the place for a quick bite to eat. I had begun my meal at a quarter past one, and at a quarter to three I had not had my coffee, yet there had not been a moment of delay in the service. The restaurant oozes solidity and generosity from all its pores.

Closed: *Saturday and Sunday and during the month of August*
Métro: *8 Ledru-Rollin* **Map: 5**
Approximate price: *200F*
Fixed price menu: *145F*

Astier
44 rue Jean-Pierre-Timbaud
Tel: 43.57.16.35

A beautiful dining room between large windows closed with roller blinds at night and a buffet; linen napkins patterned in pink and white and linen tablecloths; on the right a genuine antique Thonet coat-rack. At half past nine the dining room begins to fill up slowly with guests who seat themselves on handsome old-fashioned bistro chairs with an elegant wooden framework. The lamps have large Tiffany-style glass shades, giving an agreeably subdued light. Beautiful porcelain plates and heavy cutlery add up to the impression of a thoroughly well-established restaurant where people of all ages and kinds come to eat well and in prodigious quantity. In this neighbourhood virtually without tourists, you would not expect – as happened one evening when I was there – a flower girl making a quick round of all the tables and disappearing within a minute – like some sort of apparition.

The four-course menu costs 120F. For this price you can choose one of ten entrées from the bill of fare, handwritten daily. On a given day, for instance, there are two salads, one of chicory (*endives*) with cheese and walnuts, and one of curly *frisée* lettuce with roasted goat's cheese of the *crottin-de-Chavignol* variety, a small, dry, rather compact cylinder with a pronounced flavour slightly enhanced by roasting. Then there are – in season – green asparagus, four or five thick stalks with a tasty vinaigrette, a fish terrine with *beurre blanc*, a rabbit terrine and a terrine of chicken livers, all home-made by the passionate *patron-chef de cuisine*, Michel Picquard, as is the dish of steaming ravioli served in a creamy basil sauce.

I ate a mixed lettuce salad with smoked goose sausage: crisp and well-flavoured with five or six generous slices of sausage. My main dish was hot *tête de veau*, calf's head with an enormous boiled potato sprinkled with fresh parsley. A classic dish for when you are really hungry and do not have to watch your waist-line . . . or decide not to do so just for once – it's worth it!

Other items on the menu: salmon fillet with tarragon sauce; rabbit with mustard sauce and fresh noodles; braised flank of veal with tomato sauce, plus another six main dishes. The wine cellar is well-stocked with a good many items at under 100F a bottle. There is an extensive selection of red and white wines from the northern Rhône valley (Côte-Rôtie, Hermitage . . .), and from Burgundy including Chablis. The Chablis *premier cru* Vaillon, produced by Daniel Defaix, has a gleaming golden colour, enhanced by the beautiful wine glasses, pale tablecloth, and subdued lighting, as I noticed on an adjacent table one evening.

The cheese platter is magnificent and comprises as many as twelve different kinds, most of them ripened (*affiné*) in **Astier**'s own cellar, with among them a Saint-Nectaire *appellation controlée*, and a Boulette d'Avesnes, a strongly smelling and tasting herb-flavoured cheese from northern France, in the shape of a pear with a crust dipped in beer. And of course the small goat's cheeses, sometimes personally brought by Michel Picquard from the region around the famous village of Sancerre in the Loire valley.

For dessert the menu offers *crème caramel, clafoutis aux mirabelles, aux pêches* (peaches), *aux abricots,* pastries and sorbets. I chose the prunes in Floc de Gascogne, a *vin de liqueur* composed of fresh grape juice and Armagnac, a delight for those with a sweet tooth.

Everything here is generous, well-prepared and without any superfluous trimmings – simply good food and good service, and a certain charm. As to value for money: **Astier** is certainly one of the best addresses in Paris for anybody who likes to eat with zest and gusto, and who appreciates royal portions which seem to get larger as the meal proceeds.

This is one of those places I would unhesitatingly travel six or seven hundred kilometres to visit. It is strongly advised to book at midday and evening, for Thursday and Friday nights even two days in advance.

Open: *12 to 2 pm and 8pm to 10 pm*
Closed: *Saturday & Sunday; two weeks in May, August, two weeks in December*
Métro: *3 Parmentier*   **Map: 5**
Approximate price: *180F*
Fixed-price menu: *120F*

Chez Gaston
11 rue du Plâtre
Tel: 42.77.05.09

The signboard above the entrance (fenced off by a wrought iron gate during closing hours) shows a Bordeaux-type wine bottle on the left labelled with the address and a Burgundy bottle on the right with the telephone number; in between, **Chez Gaston** in large block letters, and on a check tablecloth a plate with three slices of *rosette* (pork sausage from Lyon) and a slice of ham with a circumference shaped like the periphery of the city of Paris. The designer, a nephew of the owner of this hidden-away wine bistro in the old Marais district near the Pompidou Centre, could have used the same drawing as a visiting card for this writer, I thought.

Inside, it feels like a quaint, underground vault rather than a ground-floor room. Modern oil paintings adorn the walls here and there and some are for sale. The one I liked best cost 6300F, which is not much for a work of art, but just a bit above the budget of a writer of moderate means who passionately loves eating and drinking.

The clientèle is composed of quiet young people sometimes including girls of the nearby Studio du Marais ballet school, located on the first floor of a picturesque little courtyard at the end of the rue du Plâtre (on the rue du Temple no. 41).

Wines come from Cheverny in the Loire valley below Orléans (a Cabernet from Tessier), from the Beaujolais (a good Château de Saint-Amour produced by Odette Sirodin), and from the Mâconnais (an excellent Mâcon *blanc*). The Côte-Roannaise from Paul-Louis Lapandéry et Fils at Saint-Haon-le-Vieux near Roanne (on the Loire between Lyons and Vichy), an excellent red wine from the Gamay grape made smoother with a little Pinot Noir, is available here at 100F a bottle. You can eat a *saucisson chaud de Lyon* (a hot pork sausage – 47F) with it, or a *daube de boeuf* (beef in red wine) for 55F.

I ate here one evening for 56F: a tureen of steaming hot tripe with four good boiled potatoes which was a real delight. Gaston Balancin, the amiable *patron* of this establishment has large quantities of tripe shipped to him directly from the *département*

Ariège, north west of Perpignan where he originally comes from, and where he still has family ties. The red wine that went with this hearty and very tasty dish with lots of delicious capers (Gaston's personal touch) comes from the region around the village of Beaumes-de-Venise in the southern Rhône. This Venetian balm displays hints of red fruits like cherries and raspberries in the scent and flavour and just that hint of sweetness that suits the tripe dish wonderfully. "Nobody can tell me that tripe cannot be the greatest delicacy on earth," I jotted down in an outburst of enthusiasm, when savouring this dish.

Other hot dishes on the blackboard near the bar: *blanc de volaille aux champignons* (chicken) – 55F, *pot-au-feu en salade* (salad of boiled beef) – 35F. You can also find lamb stew or *confit de canard* (preserved duck) on offer here on some days for around 55F.

Follow the advice of the *patron* or of his young assistant Gilles when making your choice of wine (as I did with the Côtes-du-Rhône Villages Beaumes-de-Venise). Gaston also often visits the Corbières region. The red Corbières from the Montagne d'Alaric seems to be one of the best of the *appellations* and I do hope that a new supply will have arrived by the time you get there. Because on my last visit I finished the last bottle of the 1979 vintage together with Gaston. It was a great pleasure.

Open: *10.30 am to 3.00 pm and 6.30 pm till midnight*
Closed: *Sunday and Monday*
Métro: *11 Rambuteau or 1, 11 Hôtel de Ville*   **Map:** *5*
Approximate price: *100F*

Jacques Mélac – Bistrot à Vins

42 rue Léon-Frot
Tel: 43.70.59.27

Entering the rue Léon-Frot from the rue de Charonne, you will find Jacques Mélac's wine bistro on the corner of the rue Émile-Lepeu, immediately recognisable by the grape-vine climbing the façade. The grapes are used to make a small quantity of wine called "Château Charonne" which is auctioned for charity every year.

There is a small stainless steel *zinc* with a few bar stools from which an impressive array of cheeses from the Auvergne region with their appropriate guillotine-like cutting devices are in full view.

An arbitrary selection from the large mosaic of small blackboards on which the wines on offer are marked, will convey the variety available per glass of 8cl or 16 cl contents, and per bottle: Vouvray *demi sec* at 7F, 14F and 66F respectively, Jurançon *moelleux* at 8.30/16.60/76F, Chignin (a white grape variety) de Savoie at 6.80/13.60/64F, Quincy at 8.20/16.40/76F, Lirac *blanc* or *rouge* from the *patron*'s own five-hectare vineyard in the Rhône valley at 8.40/16.80/78F. A white Mâcon-Clessé, available at 8.90/17.80/83F is neither bad nor remarkably good. Even a Sylvaner from the Alsace can be had for 7.10/14.20/67F. So much for the whites. Reds on offer include a Saint-Joseph from the northern Rhône valley at 9.90/19.80/93F, some Beaujolais growths at 9.50/19/89F, of which the Morgon seemed all right without being very typical, while the Beaujolais-Villages Lantignié, a popular wine at Jacques Mélac's (7.70/15.40/72F) was rather watery with little backbone. A nice choice of little Gamay wines from secondary regions is available at small prices: Gamay du Haut-Poitou at 6/12/57F, Coteaux-du-Lyonnais at 6.30/12.60/60F, and Saint-Pourçain from the owner's home country, the Auvergne, at 6.30/12.60/60F. From the same region, a curious *vin de noix* is available at 8F a very small and 12F a small (8cl) glass, a wine stabilised with an extract of green walnuts instead of sulphur, and to outweigh the resultant astringency, unfermented must has been added. Another Gamay wine is from the Touraine: 6.30/12.60/60F. Other Loire wines: Anjou *rouge* from grower Leduc at Faye 6.60/13.20/62F, Saumur-Champigny at 7.90/15.80/74F, and Chinon at 8.30/16.60/78F. A wine rarely found in a wine bistro is the Marcillac from the south-west of France. It is available at 6/12/58F and well worth trying for its robust earthiness.

Quite a variety of *appellations*, but unfortunately here, as elsewhere, the wines on offer are not always typical of their *appellations*, so it is better to go by your palate than by any expectations you might have. And you might want to conform to local habits and order whatever wine is most in demand at the time, always a good line of conduct anywhere in Paris, by the way. Look around or simply ask one of the friendly young waiters clad in long black or blue aprons.

The choice of food is as ample as you would expect in a place that proclaims wine to be the king and food to be his loyal subject. To begin with there are about half a dozen different omelettes (bacon, raw ham, various Auvergne cheeses such as Cantal, Roquefort, *fourme* d'Ambert . . .) for about 30F. Omelettes are an old tradition of Jacques Mélac's, going back to 1977 when he and his wife opened the bistro simply with wine and omelettes. Assorted cheeses can be had on a platter for 46F. The *assiette du bougnat – sélection pour gros mangeur*, a platter of country *charcuterie* including raw ham, *fritons* (deep-fried cubes of duck or goose meat), *rillettes* (chopped pork and goose simmered in lard), *pâté* with boletus mushrooms (*cèpes*), air-dried sausage and preserved pork liver, is available at 44.50F. Any of these constituents can be ordered separately for between 20F and 27F and gherkins or butter on the side costs 1F extra. *Gésiers confits*, preserved poultry gizzards, a good side dish while sampling coarse country wines like Marcillac, is 35.50F.

There is also a hot dish, prepared at midday by Madame Mélac for about 50F, often a speciality from the central French province of the Auvergne. Be sure to arrive in good time – because even though there is an extra back room and, in summer, an open-air pavement terrace, demand keeps exceeding the space available and reservations are not taken.

I once ate trout here, simply prepared with cubes of fried bacon and garlic, an original Auvergnat recipe, which was a memorable treat, partly because the trout itself was full of flavour and not flabby as is often the case with farmed restaurant trout. Wild freshwater trout is almost impossible to come by, an excellent reason for not ordering trout dishes in most places. Another interesting fish dish is the *morue auvergnate*, dried cod cooked with crushed bay leaves, nutmeg, full-cream milk, butter and potatoes. A typical winter dish is the *truffade*, another Auvergnat speciality prepared with potatoes and fresh Cantal cheese. *Andouillette* (chitterling sausage) and other *charcuterie* from the excellent Paris *charcutier* Duval, frequently appear among the day's specialities at this wine bistro, as well as classics such as *blanquette de veau, boeuf en daube* (beef in red wine) and, a recent addition, *pot-au-feu*, boiled beef with turnips, carrots, celeriac, leek and bone marrow – quite a treat for a mere 52F!

A cup of coffee is 4F at the *zinc* and 6F at the table.

A real family bistro: ten-year-old Marie-Hélène often chalks the day's main dish on one of the numerous blackboards; Madame is busy in the kitchen, and Jacques (or "Jacky" as his wife affectionately calls him) divides his attention between his wines (also for sale by the bottle to take away), his clients, his enormous handlebar moustache and his cross-country motorcycle.

While you are in the neighbourhood, you might also want to pop in at a relatively new wine bistro (opened in May 1988), called **Ange'vin** on 24 rue Richard-Lenoir (Tel: 43 48 20 20) run by a sympathetically exuberant man, Jean-Pierre Robinot, who is serious and enthusiastic enough about wine to attend tastings in wine-growing regions hundreds of kilometres away from Paris in his scarce free time (**Ange'vin** is open from 11 am to 8 pm and closed on Sunday and Monday; there are *nocturnes* on Tuesday and Thursday, when the place stays open until 10 pm).

Open: *9 am to 7.30 pm; Tuesday and Thursday until 10.30 pm*
Closed: *Saturday and Sunday*
Métro: *9 Charonne* **Map:** *5*
Approximate price: *85F*
No reservations

Chez Robert (Restaurant Collard)
4 impasse Guéménée
Tel: 42.72.08.45

An inconspicuous façade concealing a culinary gold mine! From a faithful reader of his original *Paris Gourmand*, Jean-Pierre Imbach, who first started this guide and inspired me to continue in his footsteps, received a recommendation in a small dead-end side street off the busy rue Saint- Antoine, close to the idyllic place des Vosges. We set off to follow up this tip on a fine, brisk September morning.

At number four impasse Guéménée we found a tiny neighbourhood café. Except for a somewhat indistinct inscription on a weatherbeaten canopy, no trace of anything remotely resembling a restaurant is apparent on first sight. Once inside where the middle-aged *patron* is chatting over a glass of wine with a couple of elderly ladies, and while we sip a glass of Badoit mineral water at the formica *zinc*, we discover a display case in the far corner of the bar, obviously encasing a bill of fare to be placed outside at midday and in the evening to attract passers-by and tell them what is available. This prompts our cautious enquiry whether there is a restaurant somewhere in the back. The *patron* confirms our guess with a nonchalant grumble and without further ado briefly opens a door to let us have a glimpse of a small dining room which, set with a few round, square and rectangular tables, looks more like a cosy home than the dining room of a restaurant. On the wall behind a bench by a small buffet stocked with wine bottles, a metal sign classifies this old bistro as a *"Table de Maigret"* distinguished for the quality and authenticity of its bistro fare and commemorating George Simenon, an enthusiast for good food and the literary creator of the equally epicurean police Inspector, Jules Maigret. There are hardly more than a dozen Paris bistros which have been thus honoured.

After a last glance at the bill of fare, we decided to have our midday meal here later on. Booking was not then really necessary (it is now!), and when we returned after an hour's walk in the surrounding streets of the ancient Marais at about one o'clock, our little dining room was filling up with other guests and appetising scents were emanating from the adjoining kitchen.

The bill of fare which was handed to us by a friendly young man who turned out to be the owner's son, deserves to be quoted more extensively than usual. To start with, there are a number of different terrines all home-made and every one with an individual touch: a *terrine de lapin* (rabbit) *en gelée au vinaigre de Xérès et aux concombres* (38F), a *foie gras frais de canard* (duck) *en terrine* (92F), a *terrine de girolles* (yellow mushrooms with a very particular flavour – 72F). As always, a special addition each day that is not on the typewritten menu, such as, on my last visit, a *gâteau de foies de volaille bressane au coulis de tomate* — a pâté of chicken livers, a delicacy from the Lyon region in a delightful fresh light tomato sauce (65F). Also an old favourite: a salad of grated carrots and button mushrooms seasoned with lemon and olive oil (38F).

I was enchanted by the *terrine de girolles* – served with a vinaigrette made with walnut oil and I very distinctly tasted the unmistakable flavour of the yellow mushrooms. It was a generous helping but there was no padding of breadcrumbs or flour as unfortunately can occur all too often in this kind of mousse. On another occasion, I had the chance to try some of the other masterpieces of Robert Collard Jr: the *foie gras fraise en terrine* is a poem of delicate, smooth sweetness. The rabbit jelly (then prepared with tarragon vinegar) tasted of tarragon, cucumber and rabbit, and the *tartare de haddock*, a pink mousse of poached smoked haddock, had the full flavour of the fish, but lacked its normal toughness. In short: to all these subtle creations the opinion of the great French gastronome Curnonsky (1872–1956) still applies: *"La cuisine c'est quand les choses ont le goût de ce qu'elles sont"*, which I freely translate as "The art of cookery makes things taste of what they are". I could not think of a better compliment for young Robert Collard's works of art.

The list of main dishes offers a balanced choice of classic fare, Madame Collard's domain (Robert's mother). For 88F: *blanquette de veau à l'ancienne*, a deliciously casseroled piece of veal in a creamy white sauce with mushrooms, perhaps the best in the whole of Paris; tripe, *civet de lapin* (rabbit casserole) and *foie de veau à la crème de poireaux* (calf's liver with a leek sauce – 92F). The *entrecôte* and the *filet de boeuf* (beef) cost 85F.

Then there are some individual creations such as a *pavé de volaille aux myrtilles* – a patty of ground duck and chicken in a sauce of bilberries (90F) which Jean-Pierre relished especially, the poultry being in perfect harmony with the fragrant bilberry sauce. I had ordered the *tripes à la quercynoise* on that occasion, tripe simmered for a long time with tomatoes, herbs and spices in white wine and cognac which were brought to the table in a steaming earthenware tureen and, together with some steamed potatoes, provided exquisite pleasure.

There is a small but well-selected and well-balanced wine list. Jean-Pierre and I had formerly shared a bottle of a young red Côtes-de-Bourg for well under 100F, but now there is also a fine young, full-bodied Saumur-Champigny (cuvée Lena Filliatreau), that refreshing, invigorating red Loire wine priced at 110F a bottle and 72F for a half-litre pitcher. For an aperitif, you can have a simple white Sylvaner from Alsace for 50F a half-litre jug, which I prefer to the Muscadet de Sèvre-et-Maine for the same price. There is also a Cahors 1987 Château de Mercues for 75F a bottle, 50F a half-litre jug. As of old, the house wine is the Château Bellevue-la-Fôret, now a 1987, a good Côtes-du-Frontonnais from the south west of France made from the rare and characteristic Negrette grape, available as a red or *rosé* for 75F a bottle, or 50F a half-litre jug. And there is always a Beaujolais-Villages of the most recent vintage for 86F a bottle or 50F a half-litre jug and a Côte-de-Brouilly for 98F a bottle or 62F a half-litre jug.

The desserts, *tarte Tatin* (caramelized apple tart – 42F), *profiteroles sauce chocolat*, 42F, *île flottante à la fleur d'oranger* (soft meringue in an orange blossom flavoured custard – 38F) have all been prepared in the restaurant's own kitchen, a source of genuine pride to young Robert because they are all his personal creations. The *gâteau de riz* (rice pudding in a vanilla sauce of exemplary lightness – 32F) can be a bit solid on occasions, but never gluey; it made Jean-Pierre think of his parents' home, a strong recommendation in view of the enthusiasm with which he had previously talked about his mother's and grandmother's cooking skills.

"This restaurant probably has a great future ahead," I wrote in 1985. Now that Robert has taken over the reins from his father, and his mother is slowly retreating from the kitchen, he is continuing his cooking with unbridled dedication while keeping up close contacts with his guests, ensuring that the traditions of this old family restaurant remain intact in the hands of a fourth generation.

In 1991 this bistro alone is well worth a visit to Paris from even the furthermost parts of the British Isles! But booking here is now essential. There is still only room for about thirty-two people. The kitchen is open until eleven in the evening but it is sensible to telephone before ten if you want to come late.

Open: *Orders taken until 11 pm*
Closed: *Saturday midday; Sunday and Monday*
Métro: *1, 5, 8 Bastille or 1 Saint-Paul*   **Map:** *5*

Aux Tables de la Fontaine
2 rue des Trois Bornes and 33 rue Jean-Pierre-Timbaud
Tel: 43.57.26.00

Right in front of the unrivalled restaurant **Astier** (see page 101), the energetic young Patrick Jacquesin has created his **Tables de la Fontaine** on the premises of an old neighbourhood bistro. The name is derived from the rather rare, typically Parisian fountain (with a cupola carried by four ceremoniously dressed female statuettes) on the small square between the rue des Trois-Bornes and the rue Jean-Pierre-Timbaud, part of which serves as an open-air dining room for about forty restaurant guests when the weather is sufficiently indulgent.

The old décor has been thoughtfully redone without impairing the authentic charm of the original bistro. Pink and light blue linen tablecloths and napkins, lots of green plants, subdued lighting and a buffet which unfortunately no longer fulfils its role as a convivial *zinc* but which serves as a storage place for about twenty-seven wine bottles.

Under the severe supervision of the *patron*, clad in a turquoise green short-sleeved shirt, young waiters in white or pink shirts, black trousers and bow ties, busily serve a mixed clientèle of avid eaters.

The bill of fare opens with two set menus: one at 90F comprising an entrée, a main dish and either cheese or a dessert; the second one is available in three combinations and costs 75F:

you can either take an entrée and a main dish, or a main dish and a dessert or cheese.

What are the entrées available? Aside from the day's special dish (which was a delicious salad of green and red leaves, chicory, fresh peas, artichoke hearts marinated in olive oil and small chunks of smoked mackerel the last time I ate here), there are eleven other entrées such as a small *assiette des fruits de mer* (seafood), six *escargots*, *chèvre chaud pané sur son lit de salade* (warm bread-crumbed goat's cheese on a bed of salad), *gratinée de l'oignon* (onion soup), *oeuf moscovite* (poached egg with a mixed salad with mayonnaise), *saumon cru mariné à l'huile d'olive* (raw salmon marinated in olive oil).

And the main dishes? Again, there are two or three dishes of the day and another eleven from which you can choose: andouillette A.A.A.A. *déglacée au cidre* (a chitterling sausage from the well-known Paris *charcutier* Duval, intensely spiced, and certified by the Amicable Association of Authentic Andouillette Adepts); *rognons de veau à la graine de moutarde* (calf's kidneys in a mustard seed sauce); *pot-au-feu au sel de Guérande*, boiled beef served with leeks, carrots, celeriac, turnips and boiled potatoes which can be – when in season – the rare and very flavourful *rats*, a variety that derives its name from the shape of these small waxy potatoes, the *sel de Guérande* is sea salt from Brittany; preserved leg of duck *(cuisse de canard confit)*; beef stew; roast saddle of lamb and so on.

A special list of desserts offers a choice between *tarte alsacienne* (apple tart), *pruneaux au Saumur-Champigny* (prunes in red wine), *crème renversée* (cream caramel), *corbeille de fruits de saison* (a basket of seasonal fruit), a very agreeable *île flottante* (a good-sized caramelised mound of soft meringue floating in a vanilla custard), and various sorbets.

The fully-fledged four-course menu for 120F gives you a choice of all these goodies, plus an assortment of three cheeses, for example, Camembert, Emmenthal and *chèvre* (goat's cheese).

The wine list offers an extensive choice. The Bordeaux region is represented by nine wines from vintages as far back as 1975 (180F) and as young as 1985 (88F) while most of the fourteen Burgundies including a white Mâcon-Villages for 80F (50F a half bottle) come from the shipper Joseph Drouhin and cost between 70F and 260F. The northern Rhône is represented by some 1986 Côte-Rôtie for 190F, 200F and 600F. Aside from some Loire wines from producers unknown to me, there is a pure, wholesome and elegant 1989 Chinon from Gérard Spelty at Cravant-les Coteaux for the very reasonable price of 75F. A 1985 Cahors Clos Siguier from the small grower S. Bley at Montcuq for 75F (45F a half bottle) may be well worth trying, too.

If you stick to the two or three-course menu you can have a complete meal with good wine and a nice cup of coffee (7F) for less than 150F. If you arrive in the evening and do not find a table at **Astier** across the street, you can still easily get away here for less than 200F for the four-course menu including wine and coffee. The food is exceptionally good here – **Astier**'s chef-proprietor Michel Piquard eats here every afternoon (and evening) after he has finished work in his own kitchen, and I have recently had a superb *tête de veau sauce ravigote* (calf's head with a vinaigrette enlivened with mustard, capers and gherkins) served with delicious boiled vegetables (celeriac, leek, carrots, turnips).

Booking is essential for lunch while it is usually quieter in the evening.

Open: *Orders taken until 10 pm*
Closed: *Saturday at midday and Sunday all day*
Métro: *3 Parmentier*   **Map:** *5*
Approximate price: *140F*
Fixed-price menu: *90F*

Le Train Bleu
20 boulevard Diderot
Gare de Lyon, First Floor
Tel: 43.43.09.06

I had heard and read a lot about the station restaurant in the *gare de Lyon* near the right bank of the Seine. **Le Train Bleu** was originally the name of the train that carried Parisians via Lyon to the sunny Côte d'Azur. Nowadays, the superfast *Trains à Grande*

Vitesse leaving the gare de Lyon for the South of France are orange-coloured (the blue ones, serving the West of France, arrive and depart from the gare Montparnasse).

Two wide marble staircases lead up to the sumptuously decorated, authentic nineteenth-century dining room on the mezzanine of the station building. From outside the station, you can reach **Le Train Bleu** via a staircase *(escalier D)* or by lift.

Shortly after midday the large dining room with seating on each side of the central aisle begins to fill up with parties of four or six, a few solitary travellers, couples with suitcases, businessmen . . . Each table, covered with a spotless white linen tablecloth, is decorated with a printed menu including the wine list and leaflets advertising such facilities as the American Bar at the other end of the floor.

The service here is hierarchically organised and executed by a staff of differently uniformed servants. Orders are taken and registered in writing by several *maîtres d'hôtel* in black suits and of different moods and manners and left under a small metal saucer to be picked up by the waiters in long white aprons. This whole ceremony takes some time, and the bottle of wine that I had ordered specifying that I wanted the first glass as an *apéritif* was brought only after I had asked for it a second time.

An individual roll of white bread is brought automatically, together with a small vessel of fifty grams of Echiré butter, commercially wrapped in a printed gold-coloured aluminium foil. Echiré is a small place just north of the town of Niort in the *département* Deux-Sèvres not far from the Atlantic Ocean. On grazing land of a few thousand hectares, from the milk of about two to three thousand cows, what is reputed to be one of the world's best butters is produced, due to the unique qualities of the soil and the grasses growing there. Echiré butter does not need to be pasteurised because the cows are checked by veterinarians several times a month and all current cattle diseases have been banned from the area for decades. The butter tastes good, but is not as exceptional as I had expected.

The printed menu is supplemented by a small typewritten and mimeographed leaflet attached to it offering a choice of the day's specialities and by two fixed-price menus on a separate sheet. One "at very high speed" (*très grande vitesse*) for 250F promises to be served within three quarters of an hour and comprises fresh, home-cooked duck's liver *(foie gras)*, a piece of roast Charolais beef and the day's pastry. The other one is the standard lunch menu, including a half bottle of wine, at 195F with a *daube de boeuf provençale* (Provençal beef casserole) with oven-browned macaroni *(au gratin)* as the main dish and half a bottle of the Vin de Pays d'Urfé, a Gamay wine made from grapes of young vines of the vineyards of the Côte-du-Forez, where the excellent house wine of **Le Train Bleu** comes from.

This Côte-du-Forez, a V.D.Q.S. (*vin délimité de qualité supérieure* – wine of superior quality from specified areas) from a small region on the left bank of the Loire west of Lyon is a deliciously fruity, light, Beaujolais-type wine which is so much better than most ordinary Beaujolais wines sold in Paris or exported for that matter. To my knowledge, **Le Train Bleu** is the only Paris restaurant that has it; the owner comes from the region.

Of course, by now you have already guessed which wine I had ordered and, indeed, my bottle of the 1989 vintage was served at the right (cool) temperature (and, at my request, was put in a bucket of ice water in order to maintain this temperature during the course of the meal). Aside from being as fresh and fruity as ever, it turned out to be even more full-bodied than I had expected (I had not tasted the 1989 vintage before). It costs 95F, while the Beaujolais *crus* here cost between 130 and 150F.

The *terrine de légumes* (vegetable terrine – 50F), a composition of mousses of celeriac, carrots and of several green vegetables, is served in a creamy herb sauce. It tastes pleasant and it looks even nicer. Three young business executives who have taken the table next to mine seem to be enjoying their Champagne (available from 280F a bottle) with their *foie gras* (98F). As so often in Paris, I admire the ease and the matter-of-fact manner with which they are enjoying their anything-but-ordinary midday meal on an ordinary weekday.

Because the place is also known for its regional dishes from the various provinces along the route to the south of France and, in keeping with the chosen wine, I had ordered the *mijoté de tête de veau à la forézienne* (simmered calf's head – 135F) which was ceremoniously served from a copper pan on a trolley in a sauce with bacon and mushrooms and garnished with a commercial brand of noodles. It was good, but certainly not over-abundant.

The *petits caillés foréziens aux herbes* (40F) are two small cylinders of goat's cheese served with chervil and chives: very young, very fresh, very watery. The *plateau de fromages* (cheese platter) at the same price is probably a better buy.

Despite the presence of many waiters of different ranks and outfits (white bow ties for the young *commis*, black bow ties and white aprons for the *chefs de rang*, and black suits for the *maîtres d'hôtel*, as one of the human and less robot-like young *commis* willingly explained to me) and, despite the fact that only about one quarter to one third of the tables are occupied, it seems a rather long wait to place a second order – for cheese in this case. And there is no extra bread with the cheese, except on request if you catch the right waiter's eye. Only my wine glass is sometimes refilled unnecessarily, but with the best of intentions, I'm sure.

The coffee is good espresso and costs 14F.

There is a lot to see here: the magnificent paintings on the vaulted ceilings . . . the whole décor is rather tasteful, the service is stylish if somewhat slow and the food is correct but has not enough character to distract you from the splendid surroundings. You can be too aware that you are paying for every square centimetre of your field of vision even though, since **Le Train Bleu** is classed as an historic monument, the maintenance of the décor is entirely at the expense of the French tax payer.

The clientèle is rather well-to-do and relaxed. A meal here can be a pleasant experience if you are with a party of three or more; or again if you order the fixed-price menu at 195F. The wine list is quite extensive (seventeen white wines, six of which are Sauternes, twenty-four red Burgundies (including ten Beaujolais) and twenty-six Bordeaux from as far back as 1978 plus about twelve others, four of which are *rosés*).

Open: *Seven days a week*
Métro: *1 RER A Gare de Lyon* **Map:** *5*
Approximate price: *360F*
Fixed price menu: *195F (midday)*

Le Traversière
40 rue Traversière
Tel: 43.44.02.10

This typical old family restaurant, which has a pronounced Touraine accent in its food and wine, is to be found on the corner of the rue Traversière and the rue de Charenton, about halfway between the Bastille and the gare de Lyon.

There are wooden beams in the ceiling, the tables and chairs are of solid wood and dark wood predominates in the décor, generally giving a rustic appearance which is in keeping with the somewhat out-of-the-way location. The quiet atmosphere and the place-settings – white linen tablecloths and napkins, with wine glasses, small bunches of flowers and green plants – make me feel at home at once and strengthen the impression of a country inn.

An abundant display of fresh *langoustes* on a large round table near the wooden bar adds a festive note. These spiny lobsters are available in portions of 450 grams at 180F.

The wine list offers a mellow Coteaux-du-Layon from Anjou for 28F a glass, an ideal aperitif (the Sauternes costs 36F).

I was more in the mood for something dry and crisp, so I had a glass of Aligoté, a light, dry, slightly acidic white Burgundy which was poured by one of the friendly ladies serving here, who also brought a small bowl of green olives which went very well with the refreshing wine (18F).

I started my meal with a *terrine tourangelle*, a coarse pâté of pure pork marinated in white Vouvray wine which was served with sour cherries, gherkin, a few leaves of curly endive and some slices of good, wholesome country bread. The *andouillette de Vouvray grillée* had been cut from a long string of chitterling sausage made according to a Vouvray recipe and roasted till crisp and brown. Served with crisp fried potatoes it was good, but the whole dish was a bit dry for my taste; I would rather have had a creamy mustard sauce instead of just mustard from the yellow pot on the table.

The *terrine* and the *andouillette* are part of the 140F fixed-price menu. Other options: curly salad with bacon or chicory salad with walnuts as entrée, *gigot d'agneau grillé* (roast leg of lamb), or *cuisse de lapin dijonnaise aux tagliatelle* (rabbit with mustard sauce and noodles) as main courses.

From the wine list I chose a half bottle of 1988 Chinon Clos du Saut-au-Loup for 45F (76F the bottle) from the good wine-growers Dozon Père & Fils at Ligré. The 1986 was listed for 110/58F, and the superb 1985 for 120/65F. Other red Loire wines: a 1985 Bourgeuil at 110F, a Saint-Nicolas-de-Bourgeuil at 78/42F, and a Saumur-Champigny from the Domaine Grande Vignole for 120/65F.

Of course, there is also white Vouvray *sec* for 140F and a *demi-sec* 1976 for 200F. The famous Vouvray *pétillant* (sparkling) costs 150F *brut* or *rosé*, and 180F *demi-sec*.

My dessert, the *pâtisserie du jour*, was an open tart with prunes, and I accompanied it with a glass of the 1985 Coteaux-du-Layon Château Montbenault, produced by the group of wine-growers G.A.E.C. Leduc at Faye d'Anjou, which turned out to be a marvel of mellowness, with a seductive balance of honey sweetness and refreshing acidity.

If you prefer to eat *à la carte* (which I strongly recommend if you want to discover and enjoy to the full the richness and generosity of **Le Traversière**'s cuisine), you may want to start with the *rillettes au pot comme à Tours* (finely cut pork slowly cooked in its own fat with spices and white wine, served in an earthenware pot – 52F), with the *terrine maison au canard sauvage* (home-made terrine of wild duck – 65F), or with two poached eggs on fresh, fragrant *girolle* mushrooms covered with a thin layer of creamy *béarnaise (oeufs en cocotte)* for 60F, and continue with *haddock poché aux épinards sauce aux oeufs* (poached smoked haddock with spinach and egg sauce – 90F). A dish of *lapin de garenne*, wild rabbit, really tasting of wild rabbit, a rare occurrence in our age of deep-frozen insipidity, served with a tasty purée of turnips and with roast potatoes, is delightfully authentic and abundant for only 88F. A cheese platter might be in order (38F) before a light dessert of *oeufs à la neige* (soft meringue in vanilla custard – 35F).

A cup of coffee with or without caffeine – *vrai* or *faux*, as they aptly say in France – is available at 10F.

The wine list, in addition to the Loire wines mentioned, offers several older Bordeaux wines such as a 1960 Saint-Julien Château

Léoville-Poyferré at 450F, a 1971 Saint-Emilion Château Roudier for 300F, and a 1979 Château l'Angelus for 500F.

I enjoyed the simplicity, the solidity, the generosity and the warm hospitality of **Le Traversière**. The well-lit dining room is spacious, with room for about thirty people, and yet, with only about ten guests present, you feel as if you are in a small country dining room rather than in a city restaurant. An oasis of homeliness and real food, this *"auberge de qualité et tradition"* in the twelfth *arrondissement* of Paris is within easy walking distance of the new Opéra Bastille.

Open: *Seven days a week (until 9.30 pm)*
Métro: *8 Ledru-Rollin or 1, A Gare de Lyon*   **Map: 5**
Approximate price: *260F*

Au Volcan

62 rue du Roi-de-Sicile
Tel: 48.87.44.54

A quaint yet lively neighbourhood café and wine bistro on the corner of the rue du Bourg Tibourg and the rue du Roi-de-Sicile, just a few steps from the monumental Hôtel de Ville, bordering a small square with a few benches . . . this is what is awaiting you right off the bustling rue de Rivoli.

Why is this small oasis of conviviality, good country wine and hearty open sandwiches called **Au Volcan**? A large board behind the busy *zinc* tells you in colourfully painted letters: *"Venant des volcans d'Auvergne, Georges Besson vous apporte ses casse-croûtes champêtres"* – "Coming from the volcanoes of his native Auvergne, Georges Besson (the sympathetic, bald-headed *patron*) brings you his country-style open sandwiches". They are served on tasty sourdough bread baked by the Paris master baker Poilâne: raw cured ham *(jambon cru)*, *rillettes* (minced pork cooked slowly in its own fat), Cantal cheese from the Auvergne. The latter, for instance, may be aptly accompanied by a glass of an excellent 1988

Saint-Emilion from the Château Lassègues, a concentrated, tannic red wine, available at 14F an 8cl glass.

There is also a good, refreshing white Quincy at 9F per glass, a spicy Sauvignon from the good grower Mardon in the wine village of Quincy on the river Cher, a left-bank tributary of the Loire. Other wines on offer on a board behind the counter: a roughish red Coteaux-d'Auvergne from the Cave des Coteaux at Veyre-Monton (in Puy-de-Dome, the *département* of the extinct volcanoes), a quaffable Gamay de Touraine from grower Henri Marionnet, Sancerre *blanc* and *rosé*, a Beaujolais, and a Riesling d'Alsace, for prices between 9F and 14F a glass, augmented by 1F when you prefer to enjoy your wine sitting down at one of the tables occupied by young people engaged in lively conversations. Don't hesitate to address yourself to the communicative *patron* who runs the *zinc* around midday while a friendly, middle-aged waitress officiates in the afternoon.

If you do not feel like a slice of *pain* Poilâne with delicious *charcuterie* or cheese (20F), you might want to take just a hard-boiled egg (4F) from the small *étagère* of wire rings on the counter with your glass of wine.

I was very happy when I rediscovered this simple, hospitable refuge in the restless heart of Paris, and I spent a very enjoyable hour there with a couple of glasses of good, unadulterated Quincy, a wholesome country sandwich and a nice chat with the *patron* and some of the regulars.

Once outside, I crossed the rue de Rivoli and went down an idyllic car-free alley (rue des Barres) along the impressive church Saint-Gervais-Saint-Protais to the pont (bridge) Louis-Philippe and across the Seine to the Ile Saint-Louis for a short walk on the quiet Seine embankments (quai de Bourbon – quai d'Anjou). You might prefer to explore the old Marais district via the rue du Bourg Tibourg. In each case, **Au Volcan** is an excellent starting point.

Open: *7 am to 9.30 pm (7 pm on Saturday)*
Closed: *Sunday and in August*
Métro: *1, 11 Hôtel de Ville*   **Map:** *5*
Approximate price: *45F*
No reservations

Porte de Sèvres, Montparnasse, Denfert, Rochereau
Arrondissements 14 and 15

Le Bistrot d'André
232 rue Saint-Charles
Tel: 45 57 89 14

This bistro is the smaller brother of the **Restaurant Perraudin** in the rue Saint-Jacques (see p.37). Its *patron* is in fact the younger brother of **Perraudin**'s Marie-Christine Kervela and the formula, a 59F fixed-price three-course menu and a small bill of fare of six entrées and six main dishes, is more or less the same as that at **Perraudin**'s.

The dining area is more spacious here and the bistro was still very new when I first visited it in the spring of 1990, while **Perraudin** has been in the rue Saint-Jacques for generations.

The dining room walls are adorned with photographs of old and new Citroën models (André was the name of the founder of the Citroën car factory and a nearby *quai* on the Seine carries his name), while the lampshades and the curtains are braided with lace, making for a traditional atmosphere. Since the character and quality of the food match the restaurant's personality, it may be worth your while to make the trip to this south western part of the outskirts of Paris, not far from the fairground of the porte de Versailles. You may even enjoy comparing the food here to that at **Perraudin**'s!

The 59F menu served at midday offers grapefruit with sugar or a cheese puff pastry as entrées, a rolled and stuffed slice of veal braised in wine (*paupiette de veau sauce Bercy*) with assorted vegetables, or a traditional *blanquette de veau* (creamy veal in white wine) and a choice of fresh soft cream cheese, pastry or home-made *crème caramel*.

I had a glass of red Lirac wine for 15F as an aperitif, a green salad with walnuts for 16F as entrée, and the *gigot d'agneau et gratin*

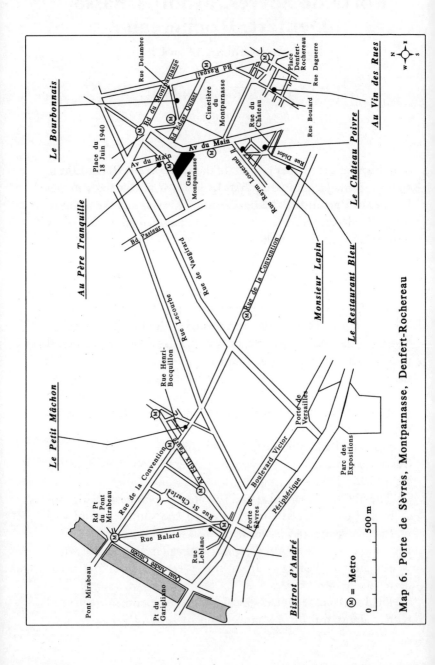

Map 6. Porte de Sèvres, Montparnasse, Denfert-Rochereau

Ⓜ = Metro

dauphinois (roast lamb with oven-browned potatoes cooked in cream) for 58F.

Cheeses are 10F (Camembert de Normandie) and 12F (Brie de Meaux, goat's cheese, Reblochon de Savoie), while desserts cost 16F to 26F (various fruit tarts, including home-made *tarte Tatin*, caramelised apple tart).

I chose the 1988 Saint-Nicolas-de-Bourgueil from the wine grower, Joël Bureau (68F). It turned out to be a good example of this light fresh, fruity, Cabernet-Franc wine from a small privileged region of the Loire valley that I always appreciate when it is a good bottle.

There are about fifteen different wines available here, a good selection from six French wine-growing areas (excluding Burgundy, but including two Beaujolais growths at 68F a bottle) at very modest prices (from 46F for a white Sauvignon from the Loire valley or a Rosé de Provence, to 104F for a 1985 Lalande-de-Pomerol). Most of them are also available in half-bottles (28F to 54F).

A cup of coffee (with or without caffeine) costs 8F, mineral water is 10 or 12F, and beer is available at 14F per 25cl. The service is feminine, informal, friendly and efficient.

This is a plain and simple restaurant with good, authentic food and a well-composed wine list which offers an ample choice of inexpensive wines (the red carafe at 8F per 25cl is only available at lunch).

Open: *12 to 2.30 pm and 7.30 to 10.30 pm*
Closed: *Saturday midday and Sunday all day. From 10 to 31 August and the last week in December.*
Métro: *8 Balard*   **Map:** *6*
Approximate price: *145F*
Fixed-price menu: *59F*

Le Restaurant Bleu
46 rue Didot
Tel: 45.43.70.56

From my hotel in the rue Delambre (around the corner from the café **Le Dôme**, on the boulevard Montparnasse), where I stay in a simple but well-kept room for very little money, it is just a quarter of an hour's walk to **Le Restaurant Bleu**. My excursion leads right through the *Cimetière du Montparnasse*, where a large number of sepulchral monuments remind me of fortified telephone booths. On the other side of this large graveyard, crossing the avenue du Maine and then walking along the rue Raymond-Losserand, near the **Château Poivre** (see page 128), I get to rue Didot. Here I find Le Restaurant Bleu with its canopy and lace curtains behind large windows between two greengrocers' shops and with a small park across the street.

There are scarcely forty places set between the walls decorated with all sorts of wooden and copper items, including a collection of Laguiole pocket knives. The dining room is also furnished with a homely *buffet* and an *étagère* full of bottles of *eau-de-vie* of all kinds. Cosy lamps with pink shades on the walls and a chandelier of two spinning wheels add to the impression of a family place in the country. There is only a handful of guests, and fragments of relaxed conversation float idly through the room . . . you have finally escaped the frantic bustling of city life and entered an atmosphere of peaceful bliss. This impression is strengthened by the friendly, unassuming manner of the young man clad in a dark red pullover, the *chef-patron*'s son, who greets you and shows you to a table.

Monsieur Elie Bousquet, who took over this fifty-five year old restaurant in 1947 from his family, originally came from the Auvergne, a fact indicated by the Laguiole knives, and borne out by most of the items on the handwritten bill of fare: *terrine auvergnate* (30F), *pâté de tête à l'auvergnate* (30F), *truffade de burons* (cheese from an Auvergne cheese-maker's hut is used in this local potato-and-cheese speciality – 75F), *tripoux auvergnats* (75F), and so on.

In October 1984, Elie Bousquet was awarded the diploma *"Mérite Amicaliste"* of the *Ligue Auvergnate et du Massif Central* for his "dedication and achievement". Another document from the *"Ordre de la Courtoisie Française"* attests to his excellent hospitality. And now and then Monsieur Bousquet himself, sporting a white chef's cap, appears in the dining room to see if everything is running smoothly.

As it most certainly was on my last visit. The *saucisse sèche à l'huile* (35F), three pieces of thin air-dried Auvergne sausage, each about two inches long, which had been preserved in vegetable oil to keep them from becoming too dry and too hard, are served nicely arranged on lettuce with good bread and a generous helping of butter. Then, after a few minutes, the *truffade* makes its appearance on a heated plate. The name of this regional dish derives from the *truffe* (truffle), a word used by local potato-lifters instead of tuber; a *truffade* is made by shallow-frying slices of boiled potatoes in lard, then adding shavings of fresh Cantal cheese (*tomme*) and garnishing that with fresh herbs, thus completing this succulent potato-cheese cake. It may sound rather heavy but thanks to the low fat content of the Cantal cheese it is light and tasty. The Cahors Clos du Pech de Jammes for 48F a half bottle (90F a bottle) with its spicy aroma and strong earthy flavour was an excellent companion to this hearty rustic dish. This dark red wine from the south west of France contains at least 70% Malbec grape, a variety also used sporadically in the Bordeaux region. The wine's quality varies considerably from one producer to another, but the one served at **Le Restaurant Bleu** is very recommendable.

Unfortunately I had to skip the board of Auvergne cheeses (40F) (one cheese dish during a meal is enough, I thought), but the *oeufs à la neige* (soft meringues on vanilla custard) which had been recommended to me by M. Bousquet Jr were just right: light, smooth, and full of flavour. Coffee (18F) is served here in an old-fashioned, almost antique filter cup. It is good and the quantity is larger than in most other restaurants with their miniature espresso cups.

My bill came to slightly more than 200F. For just 90F (a price that has not changed during the past two editions of this guide) there is a *menu auvergnat* composed of *pâté de tête* (two slices of brawn on lettuce, a good combination, served with gherkins), *tripoux* (three small rolls of sheep's tripe and lamb's trotters gently braised with herbs and spices and subsequently poached in broth, sprinkled with garlic and parsley and served with boiled potatoes and sliced carrots), a generous slice of spicy, well-flavoured Cantal cheese, and *puy marie*, equal portions of brown chestnut purée and fresh white cheese, a fine combination. The set menu is a real bargain for those who want to get acquainted with authentic Auvergne fare. Wine is available from the vineyards of Cahors, Saint-Pourçain (Auvergne) and Marcillac (south west) for between 80 and 85F a bottle, 43/45F a half-bottle.

What I appreciate here particularly is that the atmosphere, the service and the food all combine to give the impression that you are a guest in the Bousquet family home rather than having lunch in a restaurant – an oasis for hungry people in search of a peaceful welcome.

Open: *Orders taken until 10 pm*
Closed: *Saturday and Sunday*
Métro: *13 Pernety*   **Map:** *6*
Approximate price: *210F*
Fixed price menu: *90F*

Le Bourbonnais
29 rue Delambre
Tel: 43.20.61.73

A restaurant of Burgundian charm, that is the impression I gained from looking at the bill of fare in the window, and a recommendation by *Le Monde*'s Robert Courtine reassured me. I passed an evening there trying out the *oeufs en meurette*, the *coq au vin* with fresh noodles and the (rather unusual) red Menetou-Salon wine. Tables covered with white linen tablecloths, old dark wooden beams on a red-painted ceiling, and a solid buffet with an espresso machine, a basket of French bread, an impressive array of bottles of *eau-de-vie*, and a large, beautifully arranged bouquet of flowers all add up to an impression of stability and generosity.

The *patronne* warns me that both the *oeufs en meurette* (poached eggs in red wine with bacon and *croûtons* – 40F) and the *coq au vin* (75F) will be served in the same red wine sauce. Both dishes are excellent. And the red Menetou-Salon from a Loire vineyard made from the Burgundian Pinot Noir grape (grower: Marc Lebrun at Ivoy-le-Pré) is full-bodied and rather complex. It costs less than 100F and is also available in half-bottles.

There is no artificial background music and the hushed conversations of the other guests, together with the tinkling of porcelain, silver and glass, and an occasional flutter of words from the kitchen, make for a perfect acoustic environment. The focus here is on eating, and I like that.

Entrées on the bill of fare include salads: *de saison* – 25F, spinach with Roquefort cheese and bacon – 45F, *landaise:* with smoked breast of duck (*magret*), preserved poultry gizzards, stuffed duck's neck (*cou de canard*), *foie gras*, pine kernels, walnuts (*cerneaux*), and lettuce – 75F, home-made *terrines* for 38F (vegetables with cream cheese), 40F (rabbit in jelly), and a small slice of *foie gras de canard* – 80F; a dozen *escargots de Bourgogne* cost 65F and marinated salmon with dill 55F. The *persillade de foie de lapin* for 40F which I tried recently was a dish of six small fried rabbit livers on a bed of curly salad with chives and parsley and some small, crisply fried cubes of bacon. The contrast between the sharp vinaigrette and the mild sweetness of the bacon fat formed a nice background for the smooth, juicy, lightly done liver.

There are about six fish dishes (depending on fresh supply) and the main meat dishes include two with calf's kidney (100F and 135F) of which I have tried one with Meaux mustard (the variety containing coarsely crushed mustard grains) served with spinach, puréed celeriac, young Savoy cabbage and fried potatoes.

There are eight sorts of cheese on the attractive cheeseboard (40F) including Roquefort and various goat cheeses from different regions and at different stages of maturity.

Desserts for around the same price include bistro favourites such as *mousse au chocolat.*

Coffee (13F) is served with complimentary chocolates and biscuits.

Don't be frightened if you see glasses with a lurid green liquid in them. They contain the *cocktail maison* (47F), a concoction of curaçao liqueur, gin and grapefruit juice. I personally prefer a *kir maison* (white wine with either blackberry, blackcurrant or raspberry liqueur) for 20F or simply a glass of good, cool, dry white wine (Menetou-Salon from the Sauvignon grape, for instance). Another option for an aperitif is a half bottle of light, aromatic red Saint-Pourçain from grower Madame Purcigle at the Enclos de Brouilly.

About half of the guests are regulars while the rest have found his address in one of the French guide books, the *chef-patron* willingly explained to me.

Open: *Until 11 pm*
Closed: *Sunday and, in July and August, Saturday at midday*
Métro: *6 Edgar-Quinet or 4 Vavin*　　　　　**Map:** *6*
Approximate price: *260F*

Le Château Poivre
145 rue du Château
Tel: 43.22.03.68

Since 1988 this small informal restaurant on the quiet Place de Moro-Giafféri, in this sedate part of the fourteenth *arrondissement*, is frequently recommended by the *patron* of the **Restaurant du Luxembourg** (see p.32) to people who want to dine on Saturday nights when his own place is closed.

The "Pepper Castle" is run by two brothers. One is to be found behind the formica-covered *zinc* or in the dining room, while the other, sporting an impressive moustache, officiates in the kitchen.

There is a small ante-room and bar which you pass through on your way to the spacious dining room at the back, or where you might want to stop and sip your aperitif.

The dining room is tastefully furnished, coloured an agreeable pink. Large mirrors and watercolours furnish the walls, and the tables are adorned with linen cloths, while the Thonet chairs have comfortably upholstered seats.

There is a menu for 89F (served until 10 pm), giving a choice of seven entrées, an equal number of main dishes, and an option of a cheese platter or one of five desserts.

The *kir au Sauvignon* (a glass of white Sauvignon with blackcurrant liqueur) is modestly priced at 15F, while other aperitifs cost between 20 and 40F and include Pernod and various whiskies.

You can start your meal with a *salade d'artichauts aux gésiers confits* (43F), (an artichoke salad with home-preserved poultry gizzards). Another possibility is the classic *museau de boeuf à la vinaigrette* (32F), a salad of ox muzzle, which is one of the menu entrées, too (others: snails, salmon mousse, duck terrine . . .)

There is a host of classic bistro dishes on offer, such as *tête de veau sauce gribiche* (calf's head with a vinaigrette of hard-boiled egg yolks, gherkins, capers . . .), *boeuf bourguignon* (beef in red wine with bacon and mushrooms), or *poulet fermier rôti* (roast farm chicken), all around 60F *à la carte*, and available as main courses on the fixed-price menu.

From the wine list, I noted an honest uncomplicated 1989 Beaujolais, produced by Jean-Marc Meunier, and available at the very modest price (for a Beaujolais) of 75F (40F for half). Other wines (from the Loire valley) are *négociant*-bottled, and cost between 55F and 95F. There are also some fifteen Bordeaux from 70F to 520F (Château Pape-Clément, 1982, a wine rarely found in a restaurant). The house wine, a *vin de table* from the Cahors region, I was told, costs 20F per 25cl carafe, and 55F per bottle.

Desserts are typical bistro fare (*mousse au chocolat, crème caramel*) and cost around 30F. A cup of coffee is 10F.

You might want to try one of the house specialities as a main course, such as the *cassoulet maison au confit de canard* (87F), the classic casserole of beans, garlic and different sorts of meat including preserved duck, or the home-preserved *confit de canard* itself, served with potatoes fried from raw in goose (or duck) fat *(pommes sarladaises)* and garnished with garlic and a fricassée of mushrooms (85F).

Wholesome, simple and cheerful, these are the right words to characterise **Le Château Poivre**; and if you stick to the fixed-price menu and the good Beaujolais, you can have a pleasant midday or evening meal here for less than 150F, very reasonable for Paris.

Closed: Sunday
Métro: 13 Pernety   *Map: 6*
Approximate price: 180F
Fixed-price menu: 89F

Monseiur Lapin
11 rue Raymond-Losserand
Tel: 43.20.21.39

In the small streets of a little-known neighbourhood behind the Tour Montparnasse, where new buildings replace recently demolished tenements, there is an excellent opportunity to eat intimately and stylishly – perhaps on a rainy Sunday afternoon.

Monsieur Lapin has survived all the recent changes and still features its black-lacquered façade with pink ornaments and showcases full of rabbit figurines, behind which you will be welcomed by an array of white linen-covered tables with white napkins and a splendid bouquet of flowers on the buffet. Quaint table-lamps with small shades (often with a rabbit on its hind legs leaning in leisurely fashion against the lamp), and small bunches of flowers turn each table into a private dining room. Lots of paintings, drawings and photographs decorate the walls – all of them with the rabbit theme. One caricature of Lewis Carroll's famous story depicts a dead rabbit under the foot of Alice, shown holding a pistol in her hand: "Malice in Wonderland".

A deep-blue carpet and classical piano music bubbling smoothly from hidden loudspeakers in the dining room contribute to the confidence-inspiring atmosphere.

The reception is friendly, and attentively taken care of by the bearded, deep-voiced, slow-speaking partner of Monsieur Lapin (M. François Ract) who officiates in the kitchen. His face (I hope he will not take offence) did remind me a little bit of a . . . rabbit when I first saw him.

Comfortable black chairs with arm-rests and black and brown check upholstered seats, traditional cutlery and subtly decorated Rosenthal porcelain – just some more details which complete an ambience of reassuring comfort. It was not crowded that Sunday at midday and my companion and I chose a table in a small niche at the far end of the dining room where we were joined by another couple a little later.

After being presented with the bill of fare, we were pleasantly surprised with a small pot of creamy white herb cheese and some freshly toasted French bread offered as an *amuse-gueule*.

Naturally the bill of fare lists a rabbit entrée, and there is a special section between six fish (110 to 150F) and eight meat dishes (110 to 140F) featuring four different preparations of rabbit for between 9F5 and 110F.

We chose a *gâteau de lapin* (a rabbit terrine) for 62F and a well-prepared green salad with walnuts and Roquefort cheese (52F) called *méli-mélo* on the menu. A poached egg on aubergine mousse was listed for 68F, two salmon dishes and two of *foie gras* for between 98F and 150F.

The dish of the day at 98F, fried rabbit liver with shallots and mashed potatoes, happened to be just what my companion, a young lady from Bordeaux with lots of gastronomic experience, fancied. I relished a dish of rabbit stewed in honey vinegar with purées of carrots and celeriac, and a cake of grated potatoes – *pommes Dauphin*. We drank a simple Muscadet de Sèvre-et-Maine (100F) which turned out to be a perfect companion for the light dishes we had chosen. There are a number of Loire reds on the wine list, among them a 1988 Saint Nicolas de Bourgueil from the G.A.E.C. Morin at "La Rodaie" for 98F, and a 1988 Saumur-Champigny from the Château de Chaintres at Dampierre for 130F. There is also a selection of Bordeaux and Bourgogne wines from 88F to 490F. The *patron* recommends a 1988 Sancerre *rouge* from Bernard Crochet at Bué for 150F which is also available as a white for 140F.

Unfortunately, after this light but plentiful meal, we felt unable to accommodate either the assortment of cheeses (40F) or the *marquise au chocolat* (55F) from the list of desserts. Other options: ice cream and sorbets from Berthillon (perhaps the best *sorbetier* of Paris, located at 31 rue Saint-Louis-en-Ile in the 4th *arrondissement*), pastries or *mousse au chocolat*, all for around 50F.

We concluded our meal with a cup of coffee (20F) which was served with chocolate truffles.

Admittedly it is not exactly cheap at **Monsieur Lapin**, but during the week there is an attractive three-course menu at midday including a half bottle of white, *rosé* or red wine (from the Commanderie de la Bargemone at Saint Cannat in Provence) and a cup of coffee. Entrée options include *compote de lapin* and scrambled eggs with salmon, whilst there are three main dishes to choose from: roast rabbit with mustard seed, salmon in a cream sauce with chives, and rabbit liver with shallots.

Mousse au chocolat, pastry and ice cream are some of the desserts available with the fixed price menu. Its price: 200F.

I specially appreciated: the warm welcome, the stylishness of the décor, the tasteful presentation of the dishes, the impeccable quality of the food, and the comforting atmosphere of calm relaxation – all adding up to value for money.

Open: *Orders taken until 11.30 pm*
Closed: *Saturday at midday and Monday all day*
Métro: *13 Pernety*   **Map:** *6*
Approximate price: *290F*
Fixed price menu (lunch only): *200F*

Au Père Tranquille
30 avenue du Maine
Tel: 42.22.88.12

A quick telephone call in the morning to find out whether they are open and at what time. The *patron* answers with a drawn-out "*ouais*" and explains that *déjeuner* is served at one o'clock as usual without, however, divulging what it is that will be served.

It is not easy to find, this small wine bistro behind the seventy-storey pitch black Tour Montparnasse, and the busy and complex gare Montparnasse with its bustling place du 18 juin 1940 (the date of General de Gaulle's appeal to the French from London) in front where the rue de Rennes meets the boulevard Montparnasse.

Two steps down from the pavement of the avenue du Maine and a few yards further into a recess between modern apartment buildings, you are confronted with a glass door and a large picture window framed by heavy wooden beams with, on either side, one of those typical dark blue Parisian street name boards reading: "Paris XVe Arrt – place du 17 juin 1934" (undoubtedly the patron's date of birth) and "Paris XVe Arrt – place Jean Nouyrigat". No signboard with the inscription **Au Père Tranquille** is anywhere in sight.

But when you enter by the glass door, which is always open in good weather, you will see Jean Nouyrigat in person behind his counter, slicing an enormous loaf of country bread to accompany his excellent home-made terrines, or carefully and expertly mixing whisked egg white and chocolate for his well-flavoured *mousse au chocolat*.

On the wall to the left there is a large oblong photograph in old-fashioned sepia tint of the intersection of streets behind the *gare Montparnasse* at the beginning of the Sixties (then without that ugly black office skyscraper). To the right, there is a beautiful black and white photograph showing a bottle of wine with two half-filled glasses on an old-fashioned wooden table, with sunshine pouring in through an open window so that bottle and glasses are throwing long shadows on the veined table top: a mirage-like image which is more in keeping with the general feel of this place than the flashy neon signs of shops and cafés across the street.

The atmosphere is enlivened by a few regulars who are almost always at the *zinc* with a bottle or two between them, re-filling their glasses from time to time: white Saumur from the incomparable Chenin grape with a hint of acidulous sweetness in its fresh flavour. About 10F a glass.

It has often struck me that very interesting, pointed conversations of a popular philosophical nature are frequently carried on here among the regulars, in a very clear and polished French which makes them a delight to eavesdrop on, even if you don't understand half of what is being said, or to join if the fancy strikes you.

When I came in at about a quarter to one, I asked for a Saumur-Champigny, a full-bodied red Anjou wine from the Cabernet Franc grape with lots of aroma and fruit, and after my glass had been filled with a fine specimen of the *appellation* by *le père tranquille*, he went back to his work on the meal to be served shortly. When I asked for a refill, the *patron* suggested that I might want to taste something else and, without waiting for my answer, he poured a glass of cool Gamay de Touraine from the grower Henry Marionnet at Soigns in the *département* Loir-et-Cher south of Blois. I took an immediate liking to the wine which turned out to be the *patron's* favourite at that time. There is always some mellow Côteaux-du-Layon available, one of the best *liquoreux* Anjou wines and I have tasted a very attractive Chinon here recently; another one of those unrivalled red Cabernet Franc wines from the lower Loire valley.

It is time to sit down at the table! The kitchen help, an exceptionally gentle, friendly and helpful young Arab, has set the tables (there are no more than about twenty places – so booking is really essential) and the slices of terrine have been placed on metal plates by the *patron* to be distributed to the various tables. My bottle of Gamay de Touraine has already preceded me to mine. For the main dish, pre-heated plates are placed before each guest followed by an earthenware bowl of a generous portion of calf's sweetbread, spinach and *pommes vapeur* (steamed potatoes). Thereafter, three sorts of cheese, a mature Cantal and two goat's cheeses, are distributed and then the delicious *mousse au chocolat* for those who want it. The price of such a meal is very simply structured: entrée, cheese and dessert are 20F each, while the main dish is between 35F and 60F; a bottle of good wine is about 60F (10F a glass). Add about ten percent for the help of the *patron's* North African assistant (always on the bill – of course there is no additional service charge here or anywhere else in France) and your bill including a cup of coffee (5F) will come to about 160F. There is no written bill of fare or wine list, as you may have gathered from this report. Everybody just waits patiently for what Jean Nouyrigat will produce from his kitchen that day – and I have never been anything but very pleasantly surprised. As by a recent excellent lamb stew which was delicious without being the least bit heavy – a masterpiece!

Don't annoy Jean Nouyrigat, or other guests, by smoking too profusely (or at all for that matter). There are so many other, and better, things to be enjoyed in this almost secluded wine bistro – perhaps one with more individuality than any other in the whole of Paris.

And eating here is always a feast for which you should take your time. I did not leave until after four in the afternoon the last time, but then I had fallen into conversation with one of the regulars.

Open: *from about 12 to about 4 or 5 pm*
Closed: *every night and Sunday and Monday all day*
Métro: *4, 6, 13, 13 Montparnasse-Bienvenüe; exit: Place Bienvenüe*
Map: *6*
Approximate price: *160F*

Le Petit Mâchon
123 rue de la Convention
Tel: 45.54.08.62

Situated next to its more lavishly appointed and chic twin brother, the renowned **Bistrot 121**, on the corner of the rue Bocquillon, this is a "real" bistro with room for hardly forty people, not including the bar with a handful of stools where meals are also served. It has been renovated by the well-known Paris restaurant decorator Slavik, in 1925 bistro-style with art nouveau elements. Slavik also designed such places as Michel Oliver's **Bistrot de Paris** at 33, rue de Lille (Tel: 42.61.16.83), the restaurant **Jules Verne** on the second floor of the Eiffel Tower (Tel: 45.55.61.44), and the *brasserie* **Baumann-Ternes** at 64, avenue des Ternes, near the place Tristan Bernard (Tel: 45.74.16.66);   each of these a show-place serving good, although rather high-priced, food.

Slavik's design, in the case of **Le Petit Mâchon**, may lead you to fancy yourself in a hall of mirrors rather than in a restaurant (even the ceiling is tiled with mirrors), and in the toilets – of miniature dimensions – you may have difficulty finding your way out with all those mirrors around you. On the ceiling and in front of a gigantic mirror opposite the bar, pink shaded lamps with long arms twisted in snake-like shapes reinforce the fairy-tale impression.

Simple tables, no tablecloths, plastic place mats, thick glass wine goblets, white cotton napkins, pepper mills and old-fashioned salt shakers – all these are of exemplary simplicity.

Since **Le Petit Mâchon** specialises in the cooking of the Lyon region, I chose a warm salad of lamb's trotters (45F) as entrée, served with chicken livers and a hard-boiled egg. Quite an audacious dish to start with, but very invigorating and well accompanied by the fresh and fruity red Coteaux-du-Lyonnais (65F) whose coarse quality nicely counterbalanced its vigorous character as well as that of the main course which followed. This was a *tablier de sapeur* (60F), literally translated "a fireman's apron" and in fact a thin slice of fried veal tripe in breadcrumbs with a small oven-browned layer of thinly sliced potatoes, garlic and parsley. Other wines on the list which might match the fare equally well include a Gamay de Touraine produced by the Confrèrerie des Vignerons at Oisly for 80F or a Brouilly, a Beaujolais growth at 120F a bottle and 60F a carafe of 33cl. There are three more *crus* from the Beaujolais available for about the same, rather high, price. If you want to start with a glass of cool, spicy white wine, there is a Sauvignon de Touraine for 30F a 33cl pitcher and 80F a bottle.

Desserts such as a classic *gâteau de riz crème anglaise* (30F), *tarte Tatin* (caramelised upside down apple tart – 40F) and various ice creams and sorbets of Paris' best *glacier*, Berthillon, at 38F, would have exceeded my capacity after the hearty fare that had constituted my first two courses. So I finished with a cup of excellent coffee (12F) in an atmosphere of satisfaction and conviviality.

Young François, a son of the *patronne* Madame Josette Moussié, is a very good host and his sister, Catherine, admirably performs the service in the dining room, including two small glass-enclosed verandas on either side of the entrance. One last remark: the décor that appeared somewhat overwhelming at the outset, seemed to recede more into the background when, towards the end of my meal, after rain had been pouring down incessantly outside, suddenly the sun came out and its rays beamed through the glass verandas, bathing the interior in a more harmonious and friendly atmosphere.

There is a very worthwhile fixed-price menu at midday, offering, for the modest sum of 75F, a choice of entrées such as Lyon *charcuterie*; warm lentil salad with shallots and herbs (*caviar lyonnais*); seasonal salad with bacon, and fresh cream cheese seasoned and amalgamated with white wine, chives and other herbs, called *cervelle de canut*, literally silk weaver's brain, reminiscent of an ancient Lyon trade that had been introduced in the sixteenth century. Main dishes include *saucisson chaud* (hot pork sausage), *andouillette de Cambray* (veal tripe sausage) *tablier de sapeur*, and pigs' trotters. The menu also includes a *fromage du jour* (cheese).

Do try the *papiton d'oie à la mousse de foie gras* (40F), a delicate goose terrine with small pieces of *foie gras*. A selection of sliced sausage is available at 40F and more varied *charcuterie* at 50F. These dishes each constitute a small feast together with a glass of good red wine (or white Sauvignon) known as *mâchon* in the Lyon region.

I specially appreciated: the broad marble-covered *zinc* with its large, old-fashioned brass coffee machine, the hearty fare, the unpretentious atmosphere (in spite of the exuberant décor), the fixed-price menu and the excellent authentic *charcuterie*.

Open: *Orders taken until 11 pm*
Closed: *Sunday and Monday*
Métro: *8 Boucicault*   **Map:** *6*
Approximate price: *212F*
Fixed price menu at midday: *75F*

Au Vin des Rues

21 rue Boulard
Tel: 43.22.19.78

A remarkable wine bistro in many respects. First of all for its name "The Wine of the Streets". This was originally the title of a charming little book about the multiple adventures, pleasures and habits of typically Parisian wine-bibbers who daily and nightly do the round of their favourite bistros and to whom wine is as essential as the air they breathe. Its author, Robert Giraud, wrote his book in 1955. It was republished in 1983 with photographs by Robert Doisneau and Giraud has dedicated a copy of this illustrated edition to his friend Jean Chanrion, the owner of the wine bistro **Au Vin des Rues**, "who is not only proficient in serving wine, but also in drinking it for pleasure and especially for friendship . . . ".

It just so happened that one of my recent visits coincided, on March 5 1990, with the presentation and celebration (about 420 litres of wine dispensed within a few hours) of the 1989 *"Coupe du Meilleur Pot"* award to Jean Chanrion for his merits as "host of an establishment where the availability of good, unadulterated wine by the glass, selected and bought directly from the wine-growers by the *bistrotier*, who then undertakes the bottling himself, helps create an atmosphere of conviviality in which lasting friendships are likely to be forged". The terms are laid down in the statutes of the *Académie Rabelais* which, since 1954, awards the *Coupe du Meilleur Pot* every year to the best Paris wine bistro *patron*.

Jean Chanrion, whose name also appears on the façade of his small, unpretentious place on this quiet street just off the lively rue Daguerre, the site of a typical Parisian open-air street-market, modestly calls himself *"cafetier"* (café holder). In fact, continuing the tradition of the wine bistro he used to run until 1987 in the 15th *arrondissement*, he also offers a complete four-course meal every day at one o'clock, and dinner every Wednesday and Friday at nine o'clock. (The bistro is closed on Sunday and Monday.)

Let me begin by citing a few examples of the very ample selection of *vins des rues*: there is an honourable white 1989 Mâcon-Clessé for 6.50F for 7cl, and a refreshing 1988 Bourgogne Aligoté at 7F. Jean Chanrion's favourite, besides all the Beaujolais *Crus* of 1989 (8 – 8.50F) – he originally comes from the region – is a very good Côte-Roannaise, a red wine of the Gamay and Pinot Noir grape varieties from the Lyons region for 5F, and an honest red Côteaux-du-Lyonnais, produced by Etienne Descotes & Fils at Millery for 4F.

The ordinary Beaujolais is also available per *pot*, a heavy thick-bottomed bottle of colourless glass with 46cl contents, traditionally used in the Beaujolais region (35F). The same *"pot"* filled with wine of one of the *crus* (Regnié, Juliénas, Brouilly . . .) costs 60F. If you want some fizz in your wine, Jean Chanrion has a fruity Clairette de Die (Poulet) at 12F a glass of 12cl (75F a bottle) and a Cremant de Bourgogne (produced by Monnassier) at 16F a glass and 100F a bottle.

In addition, there is a 1988 Meursault (Narvaux) at 140F a bottle, a 1987 Beaune (Bouzereau) for 150F, a 1988 Saint-Véran, a white Mâconnais wine produced by Martin for 90F. From the producer of the above-mentioned Aligoté (Bouzereau at Meursault) there is also a 1988 Bourgogne Chardonnay for 88F.

From the Rhône valley you can sample a 1989 white Côtes-du-Rhône made of the grape variety Viognier and categorised as *moelleux* (sweetish), by Chambeyran at 130F, and a 1988 Condrieu of the same grape variety at 180F (producer: Cuilleron).

The 1987 Châteauneuf du Pape Vieux Télégraphe costs 110F, the 1986 Côte-Rôtie by Fernandez 140F, and the 1986 Côte-Rôtie Brune by Jamet is available at 160F a bottle. And there is also a 1988 Tavel made by Lanzac at 70F.

This gives you an idea of the unusually broad range of wines available at this bistro and, as there are as many different wines to an *appellation* (the official indication of geographic origin) as there are wine-growers in the region, I like to mention the wine-growers as well. So, for good measure, I will also list the names of some of the Beaujolais suppliers: the ordinary Beaujolais comes from Chaffanjon, the Regnié and the Brouilly both are supplied by Ruet, the Saint-Amour by Spay, and the Juliénas by C. & M. Jougert.

The blackboard on which the *patron* will chalk the menu every day also features a "motto of the day", such as *"La merle qui a bien hiverné, en mars a sa nichée"* (a well-hibernated blackbird will have his nest in March), and your attention is drawn to the fact that a certain Niepce (inventor of photography) was born two hundred and twenty-five years ago today.

Today's menu gives a choice of starters – *radis maraichaires beurre demi-sel* (red and white garden radishes with lightly salted butter), *terrine beaujo* (a terrine in the style of the Beaujolais region), *salade de lentilles ou de haricots* (lentil or bean salad), and home-made *jambon persillé maison* (ham in a white wine jelly with parsley) at 25F each.

The main dish is *saucisson chaud Bobosse* (hot Lyons pork sausage from the famous *charcutier* René Besson, nicknamed Bobosse, at Saint-Jean-d'Ardières near Belleville, just some forty kilometres north of Lyons in the northern part of the Beaujolais region), and costs 45F. In general, the main dish costs between 40 and 65F and can be a *pot-au-feu, blanquette de veau* (creamy veal stew), *gras double* (a Lyons speciality: a stew of sliced ox tripe with onions, white wine, vinegar and parsley), or a *vrai poulet de Bresse maison* (a genuine farm chicken from the Bresse region near Lyons, prepared in the house style – 65F). In short: authentic bistro fare made from top-notch primary ingredients with strong Lyon accents.

There is a *plateau de fromages assortis de nos régions* (assorted regional cheeses) at 30F, a *fromage blanc crème* (fresh soft cream cheese) at 20F, and several desserts such as *mousse au chocolat, tarte au pommes* (apple tart), and *profiteroles vanilles* at the same price. The espresso coffee is served with chocolates and costs 10F. So you can have a solid, four-course meal here with a *pot* of authentic Beaujolais wine and coffee for around 150F, which is one of the best buys in Paris wine-bistro land.

There are a few regulars around the marble *zinc* with their *pots*, nibbling at some *charcuterie* while the few formica tables are set with red and white check place-mats and generous napkins by "Jojo", the dark-haired young girl who helps in the kitchen and in the small dining room, taking orders for wine. The cutlery is distributed around one-thirty and Jean Chanrion subsequently passes quietly by every table to take the orders for the food to be served.

The *terrine beaujo* comes in a huge oval earthenware vessel from which you take as much as you like. The white bread, which is automatically present on every table, is crisp and tasty. The portion of sliced hot sausage is generous and equally generously garnished with warm potato salad and lots of raw onion rings.

Everything here is carefully thought out, well prepared, adequately presented, rich, delicious and generous, and it goes without saying that the place is filled to capacity by the time the first entrées are being served. Book in advance by telephone if you want to be sure of enjoying the genuinely Parisian atmosphere and the flavourful and copious fare at **Au Vin des Rues**.

Open: *11 am to 10 pm; midday meal at 1 pm; dinner at 9 pm on Wednesday and Friday only*
Closed: *Sunday and Monday, and August*
Métro: *4, 6, 3 Denfert-Rochereau*   **Map:** *6*
Approximate price: *140F*

Le Zinc

There are very few of the original tin-covered bars left in Paris. During the German occupation just about every metal object, including the legendary bar surfaces, was confiscated and turned into armaments. Only a very few authentic "zincs" were spared but the expression "zinc" lives on all the more persistently, despite the fact that the object so designated is frequently covered with copper, brass, wood, ceramics, formica or whatever. So "zinc" is really more an expression for a typically Parisian form of conviviality: a glass and a chat among friends standing at the bar . . . a quick breathing space, a short interruption of the daily hustle and bustle, perhaps a *baguette* with Camembert or ham or pâté before going on. All this forms part of what "zinc" means to Parisians.

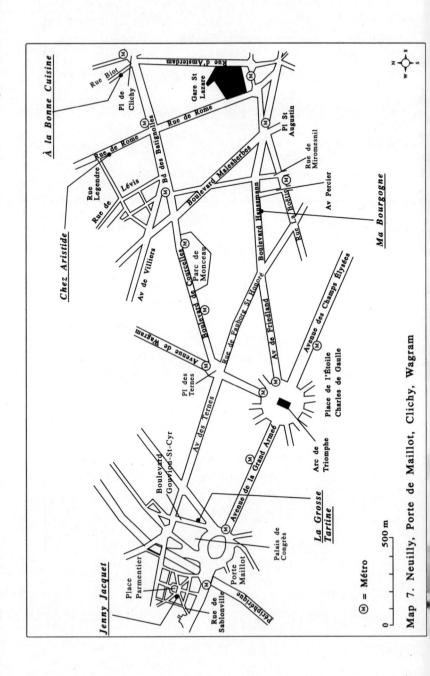

Map 7. Neuilly, Porte de Maillot, Clichy, Wagram

Neuilly, Porte de Maillot, Clichy, Wagram

Arrondissements 17 and Neuilly

Aristide
121 rue de Rome
Tel: 47.63.17.83

In a rather bleak and barren part of the rue de Rome, with the railroad tracks issuing from the gare Saint-Lazare on one side of the street, a veritable jewel of simple, wholesome Paris gastronomy is set on the ground floor of an otherwise inconspicuous building. A glance at the menu (posted on the outside as is obligatory in France) reveals the rather extraordinary pledge of the owners, Philippe and Viviane Siegrist (the name is of Swiss origin) to provide a *cuisine* of fresh produce (no canned or deep-frozen products) prepared only with butter and goose fat.

To my knowledge, **Chez Aristide** is not listed in any of the numerous guide books which claim total coverage of all worthwhile eating places in Paris. Nevertheless, the place is almost filled to capacity when I arrive there on a dreary spring afternoon around one o'clock after putting myself in the right mood for a sumptuous meal by walking around the food market stalls of the nearby rue de Lévis between the rue Legendre and the intersection of the avenue de Villiers (*métro* station of the same name) and the boulevards de Courcelles and de Batignolles.

My friend Jean-Pierre Imbach and a regular table companion of his are already enjoying their *pot de rillettes porc et oie*, an earthenware pot of pork and goose cooked in their own fat with herbs and spices which can be spread on slices of bread rather like a pâté, and I am only too happy to join them. The tables here are well spaced and there is a large service table in the centre of the dining room with vessels of pâtés, terrines and the like. On a separate table, a magnificent bouquet of flowers is displayed. The service is traditionally and discreetly performed by young waiters in long white aprons; the entire interior of this old restaurant, dating from 1893, is that of an authentic bistro.

While the *rillettes* serve as an introduction to **Aristide**'s fare, we each choose a different entrée from the variety of sixteen offered. As I savour my *oeufs en meurette* (poached eggs in a thick sauce of red wine with bacon and mushrooms, a perfectly authentic Burgundian speciality for 42F), Jean-Pierre enjoys his *salade de trois haricots* (a salad of white, red and green beans seasoned with good vegetable oil while still warm, which is then fully absorbed by the beans – 40F). The *champignons à la grecque* (mushrooms cooked in a coriander-spiced marinade of oil and white wine, served cold as a salad – 42F) of our third table companion are also meticulously prepared and generously served, a fact which deserves special mention in view of the numerous insipid concoctions of tinned mushrooms with a commercial vinaigrette served in too many well-advertised Paris restaurants.

To have such well-prepared dishes served so generously in such a congenial atmosphere is wonderfully satisfying. Everybody around (every table by now is taken) is so obviously enjoying their food and drink that one feels genuinely happy and relaxed to have the good fortune to be here.

The wine, a Sancerre *rouge* 1988, a light fruity red Loire of the Pinot Noir grape (140F) is an easy partner for just about any dish and a perfect wine for midday. **Chez Aristide**'s rather extensive wine list comprises about eighteen different Bordeaux châteaux of vintages not further back than 1983 at prices ranging from 85F (Château Beaulieu 1986) up to 390F (Château Branaire-Ducru 1983, *4ième cru classé*). The Bordeaux selection recommends itself for a more elaborate dinner while there is also a simple 1985 Cahors Château de Haute-Serre at 98F and an honest Coteaux de Lyonnais, a simple light red wine of the Beaujolais type for the friendly price of 55F.

The *andouillette 5A* chitterling sausage approved by the *Association Amicale des Amateurs d'Authentiques Andouillettes*, (the Society of Admirers of Authentic Chitterling Sausages) reputed to be the best in Paris, and served here cooked in Sancerre wine and accompanied by a *galette de pommes de terre* (potato pancake) is a real treat and those who are not accustomed to this dish should go and try it first at **Aristide**'s. The old-fashioned *blanquette de veau* (veal in a white wine sauce – 85F) and the *canette de Barbarie rôtie* (roast duckling – 88F) from the short list of today's special dishes, reveal themselves as entirely satisfying to my companions.

It is worth mentioning that the fresh oysters offered here are supplied by the reputed breeder Gillardeau at Marennes, just north of the Gironde estuary in the *département* Charentes-Maritimes. The *spéciales No 3* cost 67F per half dozen (No 3 indicates that they weigh about 60 grams a piece while *No 1 spéciales* should weigh 100 grams).

Other main dishes on the bill of fare include: three beef dishes from 86F (*entrecôte grillée*) to 118F (*filet de boeuf sauce poivre* — fillet of beef with pepper sauce), a *carré d'agneau rôti* (rack of lamb) for two at 188F and a *confit de canard pommes à l'ail* (preserved duck with garlic potatoes) for 88F, as well as four sole and two salmon dishes for between 98 and 120F.

Due to the abundance of our entrées and main dishes, we unfortunately had to skip the cheese platter (35F) and content ourselves with delicious *mille-feuilles* (puff pastry) for 42F, one of the six or seven desserts offered besides nine ice creams and sorbets.

I specially appreciated: the spaciousness and solidity of the dining room, the impeccable service, the excellent quality and generosity of the dishes, all combining to create a genuine old-fashioned bistro ambience, difficult to find in the Paris of the nineties.

Closed: *Sunday*
Métro: *2 Rome or 2, 3 Villiers*   **Map: 7**
Approximate price: *280F*

A la Bonne Cuisine
17 rue Biot
Tel: 45.22.54.35

The interior of this small restaurant just off the crowded place Clichy remains neat and conventional, as described in earlier editions of this guide. The old-fashioned benches along the walls are still there, the tables are covered with wholesome white linen tablecloths and linen napkins of sufficient size are provided.

The bill of fare still features traditional classic French cuisine but it would be a little more difficult now to accord the food itself the qualification with which Jean-Pierre Imbach, the author of *Paris Gourmand*, the precursor of this guide, praised it in 1982: "Everything at **La Bonne Cuisine** is prepared straightforwardly and in keeping with tradition. It would take no more than just a little spark of genius, and there would be genuine perfection . . .". While I once agreed one hundred per cent with Imbach's conclusion, my latest meal at **La Bonne Cuisine**, although still a predominantly pleasant experience, has taught me that Monsieur Loize, still the same *patron-cuisinier*, has abandoned the road toward perfection and has changed over to that of commercial success.

The menu is now partly bilingual (French–English), a feature that may be helpful for English-speaking visitors, and the place regularly caters to Frantour, for example, a Dutch–French tour operator.

There is still a fixed-price three-course menu (not marked in English by the way) for 68F at lunchtime only (this was 65F in 1985). The *sardines fraîches grillées* which I had enjoyed so much at my first visit, have only gone up by 1F in five years (they are now 36F) while the lamb's kidneys in mustard sauce, a house speciality, are 56F now (48F in 1985), a very modest increase indeed.

So, while the quality has not risen during the past five or six years, neither have the prices (or only marginally so) which is a remarkable achievement.

I chose the fixed-price menu this time (which gives a choice of four standard entrées, such as *oeuf mayonnaise* and vegetable soup, five *plats garnis* such as *endive au jambon* (chicory with ham) and a number of desserts. My entrée was the *terrine maison*, a few slices of home-made pâté which were adequate but no more. The *andouillette au vin blanc*, pork chitterling sausage, turned out to have burst out of its skin (which should not happen, although it does not impair the taste), while the sauce, though spicy was certainly not what you would rightfully expect to be a *sauce au vin blanc*. But then, I had arrived just after 2 pm and the kitchen had to be re-opened for this last hungry visitor. The strawberry cake was all right: a layer of fresh strawberries on a crisply baked dough with a layer of vanilla cream in between dough and fruit.

The wine I had chosen from among about twenty-five rather standard bottles (there are also some *vins en pichet* (pitchers) at 16F, 38F and 60F per half-litre) all without indication of their vintage years, was the only one listed as coming directly from the grower in Touraine, usually a safe recommendation, although the grower's name was not mentioned on the list, an omission which is always a good reason for caution! This wine turned out to be a 1984(!) *Sauvignon de Touraine* from the *propriétaire-récoltant* Jean-Claude Bodin at Saint-Romain-sur-Cher, and was heavily oxidised (56F). There are people who like the taste of oxidised white wine (it is vaguely reminiscent of the taste of dry sherry), and I took one or two glasses to let this specific taste grow on me, but it didn't. A second (half) bottle (41F) of a different but unidentifiable vintage of the same wine was rather dessicated. I recommend instead drinking Heineken beer here, as a few regular customers did at an adjacent table, a rather unusual sight in an authentic Paris neighbourhood restaurant. I've preserved a very good memory though of the Muscadet I had with my sardines and lamb's kidneys five years ago. There's still a Muscadet on the wine list (69F), and it might be as good, though of a more recent year of course.

It is very difficult to find a decent, affordable restaurant of still undeniable authenticity such as **A La Bonne Cuisine** in the vicinity of the very touristy Place de Clichy but the difficulty of obtaining a good bottle of wine annoys me.

Open: *2 pm and 7 to 9.45 pm*
Closed: *Saturday at noon and Sunday all day*
Métro: *2, 13 Place de Clichy*   **Map:** *7*
Approximate price: *110F*
Fixed-price menu: *68F*

La Grosse Tartine
91 boulevard Gouvion-Saint-Cyr
Tel: 45.74.02.77

This restaurant, recommended repeatedly by Robert Courtine in *Le Monde* for its rare specialities and its authenticity, turned out to be a real gastronomic gold-mine when I had the chance to have lunch there on a stormy summer Sunday on my way to the wine country of the Touraine.

Located right off the Paris *périphérique* (the multi-lane motorway encircling Paris) at the Porte Maillot and thus easily accessible by car, the position is doubly convenient because of ample parking facilities around and under the Palais de Congrès and the numerous adjacent large hotels (Lafayette-Concorde, Meridien . . .).

Another welcome convenience is that **La Grosse Tartine** is open seven days a week so there is no need to worry about closing days when planning your dinner there. It is, however, prudent to reserve by telephone.

When I arrived there at a quarter past twelve, the three dining areas – one near the entrance behind a small reception counter, a spacious, well-lit conservatory, and a cosy, dimly-lit dining room with an open fireplace – were still empty, as was to be expected at this early hour on a Sunday afternoon: most people come between twelve-thirty and one o'clock.

I was shown to a small table in the conservatory by a young waiter clad in a white shirt, black tie and black trousers after having been greeted by the informally dressed *patron* at the reception desk.

Instead of being asked whether I wanted an aperitif (a question which is often posed in the manner of a threat) the waiter quietly handed me the menu and the wine list. While I was studying the former, a dish of eight slices of fresh sourdough bread was placed on my table. What a pleasant surprise after the eternal omnipresent French *baguette*. And aperitifs galore on the menu: a whole column ranging from a *coupe de Champagne* (Château Charbaud) for 48F, the obligatory *kir* (33F with still wine and 46F with sparkling wine: *kir royal*) via the standard *pastis* (Ricard – 34F), Martini, Port,

Campari (36F), up to a single malt whisky (48F), and Bloody Mary (55F).

The bill of fare itself offers seven entrées around 50F plus some more expensive delicacies such as *foie gras frais de canard maison* (freshly prepared duck's liver) at 106F or *escalopes de foie gras chaud* (slices of warm goose liver) at 128F, *gambas grillées* (119F) or *saumon de Norvège fumé maison* (smoked Norwegian salmon) for 106F.

I had the *tourin des Landes* (40F), a deliciously aromatic bouillon bound with egg yolks and subtly spiced with garlic. There are quite a number of local versions of the *tourin*, a soup that is traditionally served as a fortifier to newly-weds on their wedding night in various south-western regions of France. I like the one I often make at home with lots of onions simmered in goose fat and cooked in chicken broth, but the *tourin* at **La Grosse Tartine**, the first I have ever tasted in a restaurant – it is hardly ever offered on most modern menus – was a delightful special treat. I would have preferred some more garlic in it, and the proprietor later on advised me to ask for just that when ordering, because the low level of garlic of the standard *tourin* at **La Grosse Tartine** is a concession to "modern" customers' taste. The hearty sourdough bread is an ideal companion for the tasty soup, just as the light, fruity red wine, a Cahors 1986 Château Coustarelle from Michel Cassot at Prayssac in the Lot (89F, 53F a half bottle) is for the *souris d'agneau aux poivrons et tomates* (98F). This speciality, comprising the small, much cherished, rounded muscle attached to the lower-end of a leg of lamb (called *souris* (mouse) in French because of its particular shape), roasted and wrapped in green peppers and tomatoes, is served in an aromatic brown sauce with *gratin dauphinois* (potatoes baked with cream). I don't think I have ever eaten lamb as tasty and as tender as that. And there was lots of it!

In the meantime, the conservatory dining area with its green plants and gaily-coloured parasols (swimming-pool green, aubergine purple and sky blue) had filled up with young and middle-aged couples, whole families, two young American girls (undoubtedly from one of the neighbouring hotels) who were offered an English-language menu when it turned out that their French was not quite up to deciphering the ample bill of fare: two fish dishes, three poultry dishes, all of them south-western specialities: *cassoulet* (haricot beans casseroled with preserved goose or duck, pork or lamb and sausages), *magret* (breast of duck) and *confit de canard* (preserved duck), three lamb and three beef dishes, all around 100F.

The background music (from semi-classical to ballroom jazz), which I had found a bit too prominent to begin with, blends in harmoniously with the background hum of lively table conversation, the tinkling of glassware and the clicking of knives and forks.

Everything combines into a harmonious whole: the tablecloths and napkins, the tiled floor, the semi-circular sliding glass roof which can be opened and closed within six seconds, the informal, unpretentious and yet very attentive service . . . and the speed with which various drinks are served: wine, beer (27F for a bottle of 33 cl), mineral water (17F), and of course the thoroughly wholesome and delicate food prepared by the excellent cook, Madame Odette Pilmis, assisted by a staff of three or four young men in a kitchen which, rather like a huge aquarium, can be viewed through a large picture window framed by all sorts of green plants and trees.

Before having my cup of excellent espresso coffee (17F), I tried the *tourtière landaise chaude* (43F) which turned out to be a thin slice of warm apple tart made of puff pastry. Very carefully prepared and a real treat, especially for those who prefer apple sweet rather than sharp.

There are also *profiteroles au chocolat* (49F), a fruit salad (42F), a *gâteau au chocolat amer* (bitter chocolate cake – 43F) as well as sorbets and ice cream for 42F.

And, of course, there is an *assortiment* of cheeses for 41F.

A very good restaurant where simplicity, authenticity and excellence meet!

Open: *Seven days a week*
Métro: *1 Porte Maillot*   **Map:** *7*
Approximate price: *290F*

Jenny Jacquet (La Truffe Noire)
2 place Parmentier
Neuilly
Tel: 46.24.39.42 and 46.24.94.14

This restaurant stretches the limits of this book in more than one respect. Located just beyond the city limits of Paris (although a mere five *métro*-minutes from the Arc de Triomphe) the cost of a meal here is well above the highest elsewhere in this guide.

But as there are a number of restaurants described here with the advice that, in my opinion, they are worth a journey from even the most remote part of the British Isles, the *extra-muros* location of Jenny Jacquet's eating place should certainly not preclude its listing here. In the intrinsically difficult judgement of value for money, if the emphasis is laid upon sheer quality then Jenny Jacquet's is perhaps the restaurant offering the best value for money in the whole guide.

In my description of Jenny Jacquet's former place in the rue de la Pompe in the sixteenth *arrondissement*, I wrote in 1985 that this bistro formed the yardstick by which I judged all the other establishments. Nothing has changed, except the location – reason enough for an entry on **Jenny Jacquet** still being a must.

An idyllic little square, the place Parmentier in Neuilly has a rather monumental library building on one side, with six streets radiating out from this small *place de l'étoile* just outside of the Paris *périphérique*, linked to the Arc de Triomphe in the centre of the real Place de l'Etoile by nine hundred metres of the avenue de la Grande Armée; (and by a short *métro* trajectory with just one intermediate stop). On one of the street corners (rue de Sablonville) you will find the real star of the Place Parmentier: **La Truffe Noire** of master chef and restaurateur Jenny Jacquet.

Outside, awnings announce his name; inside, an oblong dining room, a small *salon*, and a glass-encased terrace are awaiting you.

The reception is in the hands of Madame Chantal Jacquet.

The bill of fare has been composed as carefully and intelligently as the extensive wine list. Nine *"petites entrées"*, five or six fish dishes, five meat dishes often comprising such specialities as veal kidneys, breast of duck (*magret de canard*), and sweetbreads, six desserts, about thirty red Bordeaux wines, a dozen red Burgundies, about six red Loire wines, some *rosés*, almost thirty white wines half of which come from the owner's native Loire valley, and more than a dozen different Champagnes.

My escort on a memorable evening at Jenny Jacquet's opted for the *éventail* (fan) of *courgette et sa mousse de poivrons en coulis mediterranéen* (75F) while I chose the *artichauts bretons en terrine* accompanied by a *sauce onctueuse de crustacés* for the same price. Two entrées which, in addition to being beautiful to the eye, turned out to be exquisite to the palate. The creamy quality of the pale sauce is playfully demonstrated by two treble clefs carefully "drawn" with dark sauce on either side of the slice of spicy artichoke terrine. If the sauce was any less consistent, the pattern would quickly be ruined. These creations are not just pretty and full of flavour, but served in very generous portions on large octagonal porcelain plates. Not a trace of the visual substitutions of *nouvelle cuisine*. On the contrary: as a generous supplement each dish is "decorated" with a genuine giant prawn! This was the generous spirit which had already impressed me in Jenny Jacquet's convivial bistro in the rue de la Pompe!

The main dishes: *sandre* (pike perch) *en mousseline* with the famous *beurre blanc comme en val de Loire*, one of Jenny Jacquet's specialities; connoisseurs are of the opinion that it is the best butter sauce with shallots and white wine outside Rosiers-sur-Loire. No wonder: Jenny Jacquet has been trained by the uncontested *"roi du beurre blanc"*, Albert Augereau, former chef of the famous **Jeanne de Laval** restaurant at Rosiers, who unfortunately passed away in 1985.

While my partner was enjoying her delicate fish mousse, I amused myself with three slices of fresh cod rolled up in lettuce leaves with boletus mushrooms (*cèpes*) and bone marrow in a red Saumur-Champigny wine sauce, an interesting and surprisingly harmonious combination and in my humble opinion a monument to the inventiveness of this master chef.

As I remembered from Jenny Jacquet's bistro on the rue de la Pompe, the steamed potatoes are served from a special copper pan.

Main dishes of this level of quality and presentation cost between 110 and 130F. Sometimes there will be more expensive dishes in which truffles are used. After all, before Jenny Jacquet took over this restaurant, it was called **La Truffe Noire** and the name is still on the building, in the telephone directory and on the menu, in conjunction with the new owner's name. An example: a fish dish with truffle chips for 175F. The bill of fare is not without its touch of poetry; as with the *suprème de daurade grise en écailles de truffes* – fillet of black sea bream with truffle scales. The *daurade grise* is considered to be less good than the red sea bream and usually less expensive. Both varieties are much more common and considerably lower priced than the *daurade royale* or *"vraie daurade"* which is found only in the Mediterranean while the other two varieties are North Atlantic fish. Many another restaurateur might simply put *"suprème de daurade aux truffes"* on his menu, thus perhaps unwittingly creating the impression that a dish of the rather rare *daurade royale* with truffles was on offer. Not so Jenny Jacquet who has developed into a veritable master in the art of using truffles, witness a creation of his which I had the pleasure of tasting recently: a *terrine de poireaux aux truffes fraîches* (85F). The green leek leaves, embedded in a light yellow vegetable mousse, are generously and artfully interlaced with truffle shavings and the whole is served in a well-flavoured green sauce. On the same day there was a whole truffle of thirty grams *"en surprise"* on offer for 220F.

Jenny's son has recently started to work as wine waiter advising knowledgeably but unpretentiously about which wine to choose with your meal. And to my utter satisfaction, in this restaurant the tin capsule is cut off just below the collar around the neck of the bottle to prevent the wine from coming into contact with the tin before reaching the glass. A detail worth mentioning: I know of less than a handful of restaurants (just one other in Paris) where this excellent rule is followed. Usually the capsule is cut off above the collar – to spare the restaurant's tablecloth rather than the wine.

In our case the choice of the wine was not difficult. As one of our dishes was prepared with red Saumur-Champigny from Château de Targé (1988), we chose the same wine to go with our meal (120F). Another Saumur-Champigny has recently appeared on the list: the Clos Cristal of the Hospices de Saumur (1988). According to Jenny Jacquet, it is even better than the Château de

Targé, and certainly hard to come by. It is not being exported and, on a visit to Saumur in September 1990, I did not manage to obtain one single bottle as the 1988 vintage was sold out and the 1989 vintage had not yet been bottled. So I have to take Jenny's word for it, not difficult as he is known to be a great connoisseur of this light Loire red.

At this point, it occurs to me that I have forgotten to mention the glass of white wine we enjoyed by way of introduction to all these wonderful works of culinary and oenological art. Even though our confidence in the restaurateur, the best of all possible aperitifs, had already been firmly established, we chose a glass of cool, mildly sweet and richly flavoured Coteaux-du-Layon Chaume, Château de la Roulerie 1988, for 26F. But if inclined toward a dry white wine to start off a festive meal, don't fail to order a bottle of the incomparably light, lively and refined Jasnières 1985 from the excellent wine grower J. B. Pinon at Lhomme, about fifty kilometres north of the city of Tours. It is only 150F and will leave a memorable and indelible impression . . . as long as the vintage lasts. You can then have the Chaume with your dessert; there are six of these priced at 50F, of which I can especially recommend the *duo de crêpes chaudes garnies de pommes caramelisées* (pancakes with caramelized apples).

But before that, there is a *choix de fromages affinés,* ripened in the cellars of La Maison du Fromage by Maître A. Quatrehomme (62, rue de Sèvres, Paris VII, tel: 47.34.33.45) which certainly deserves all the attention of devotees and connoisseurs (both the *choix* and the *Maison*!). With the cheese, a choice of bread, brown and white, is offered. A cup of good coffee (espresso of course) is 16F.

I recommend this restaurant to everyone because the dishes here are models of careful preparation, correct presentation, inventiveness and generosity, and the richly endowed wine cellar is exemplary in its composition and level of quality. For each *centime* you spend here, thirty-five to forty-five thousand per person (count on a bill of around a thousand francs for two if you eat *à la carte*), you get more than anywhere else I know.

But there is also a three-course menu for 220F offering a choice between four entrées: six prime oysters – poached eggs in red wine sauce – avocado mousse – a *ballotine* of poultry with coriander-spiced vegetables. The main course, one of four fish and three meat dishes, can be followed by cheese or one of four desserts (sorbets, *crème brûlée* . . .). So skipping the aperitif and ordering one bottle of wine you can get away with about 600F for two, and your satisfaction will be none the less for that – although I would find it rather difficult to resist all the other solid and liquid temptations on offer here.

Booking, by the way, is absolutely essential . . . several days in advance preferably.

Je t'admire et j'adore ta cuisine, Jenny Jacquet!

Closed: Saturday and Sunday
Métro: *1 Porte Maillot*   **Map:** *7*
Approximate price: *400F*
Fixed price menu: *220F*

Ma Bourgogne
133 boulevard Haussmann
Tel: 45.63.50.61 and 45.63.56.62

Louis Prin, the small mustachioed, fifty-two-year-old (but younger looking), *patron* of this rather civilized wine tavern was awarded as early as 1962 (when he must have been twenty-four) the *Coupe du Meilleur Pot* by the *Académie Rabelais* for his merits and accomplishments as tenant and head of that sacred institution which is the Parisian wine bistro. In fact, Louis Prin runs a pleasant, well-lit establishment on the broad and stately boulevard Haussmann that has more the spacious feel of a *brasserie* than the cosy, dense atmosphere of a wine bistro. But besides the usual (for a *brasserie*, literally meaning brewery) draught beer, Kanterbräu from Alsace and Carlsberg from Denmark, and simple snacks, a choice of wines directly from the growers can be sampled by the glass.

At midday an attractive *menu du marché*, prepared with fresh produce, is on offer and served at two tables with comfortably upholstered benches near the counter and on the glass-covered pavement terrace (seating about twenty-four people). On a recent visit the choice was offered of two entrées (fillets of marinated herring with potato salad – 27F, and celeriac with sauce rémoulade – 20F), and the main dish was a *navarin printanier* (lamb stew with spring vegetables) for 61F. For 19F you have the choice between a number of cheeses including Camembert, Cantal, Comté, Pont l'Evêque, Brie de Meaux, Saint-Nectaire, *fourme*, while the *petit mâconnais*, a goat's milk cheese, costs 26F and an assortment of cheeses is available for 28F. Desserts? There is a good fresh pastry for 25F and the *mousse au chocolat* is 22F.

Wine is served in beautiful glasses etched with an eight-pointed star. I sampled a few of the wines carefully marked on a large board easily visible from the comfortably spacious brass counter. To begin with, there is an agreeable 1988 Mâcon *blanc* produced by M. Michel at the wine village of Clessé and, like most of the wines in a real wine bistro, bottled by the *patron*. The Gamay du Haut-Poitou at 5.80F per 8cl glass, the cheapest wine on offer, is a fresh, upright summer red, full of flavour. Unless one or other happens to be sold out you can sample here almost the whole gamut of Beaujolais growths (there are ten altogether now, with the Regnié as the latest promoted to the rank of *cru*) as I did one afternoon under the able guidance of the excellent wine waiter who, after twenty years at **Ma Bourgogne** now has his own place, **Le Relais Beaujolais**, in the ninth *arrondissement* (see page 83). The prices range from 25F for a 25cl pitcher (which comes to about 8F per small glass) of ordinary Beaujolais to 34F for a 25cl pitcher of the Moulin-à-Vent.

The prices of Burgundy wines are in general far too high for them to be dispensed by the glass while their quality is questionable more than nine times out of ten. So the offer at **Ma Bourgogne** is limited to a tasty, fresh Marsannay *rosé*, a pink wine from the northernmost part of the Côte d'Or which, in good years when made by a good grower, can be counted among the best *rosés* of France. At the cost of a mere 8F per glass, the 1987 was a bit meagre, not very fruity but still fresh and agreeable in 1990. Then there is a Marsannay *rouge*, recently promoted to the status of *appellation controlée*, the highest rank in the hierarchy of official French wine nomenclature, which is available at the still modest price of 110F a bottle.

Between wines, why not try a slice of hearty, fragrant sourdough bread supplied by the excellent Paris baker Poilâne and covered with a few slices of *rosette du Beaujolais* (large, dry pork sausage – 16F) or *jambon du Morvan* (smoked ham – 20F) or spread with *rillettes de Conneré* (minced pork cooked in its own fat, a speciality from the Sarthe, a region around Le Mans), *pâté de campagne* (15F) or *terrine maison* (home-made terrine – 16F). If you want something more substantial, try the *saucisson chaud pommes à l'huile* (hot slices of pork sausage with potato salad – 47F), or a *steak tartare* (freshly minced raw fillet of beef prepared with oil, vinegar, pepper and salt and blended with onions, capers and egg yolk), a typical *brasserie* dish for 60F. The *assiette paysanne* with *rosette*, *pâté*, *jambon* and *rillettes* will be served for the modest sum of 45F.

The atmosphere is lively and relaxed, the *rillettes* are excellent, the wines are pure and honest, each one having its own appropriate character and personality. The pastry is original and delicious. And of course good coffee is available too for 4.50F a small cup at the counter and for 7F when you are sitting down at a table.

There is a more elaborate dining room in the basement.

Open: *7 am to 9 pm*
Closed: *Saturday and Sunday*
Métro: *9, 13 Miromesnil* **Map**: *7*
Approximate price: *185*

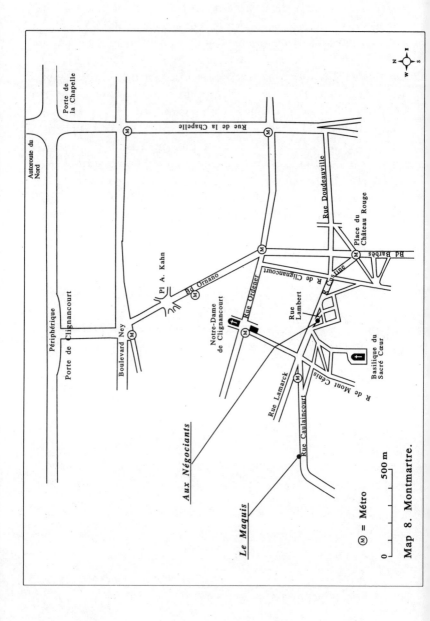

Map 8. Montmartre.

Montmartre

Arrondissement 18

Le Maquis
69 rue Caulaincourt
Tel: 42.59.76.07

An off-season weekend, when Paris is still relatively free of tourists, is the ideal time to get an impression of the gastronomic scene. On the northern perimeter of the city my travelling companion Willem and I picked out **Le Maquis** in the rue Caulaincourt in the eighteenth *arrondissement*, described in the first edition of this guide (1985). This quiet street runs in an east–west direction behind the *butte Montmartre,* which makes **Le Maquis** the northernmost bistro in this guide.

If you arrive by car from the *autoroute* Calais (or Lille) – Arras-Senlis and you follow the westward (*"ouest"*) direction into the boulevard périphérique, leave via the porte-de-Clignancourt exit and drive down the boulevard Ornano and then the boulevard Barbès, take the third street on the right (rue Doudeauville) which will lead into the rue Custine which, in turn, will run into the rue Caulaincourt after a few hundred yards. After about another five hundred yards you will find **Le Maquis** on your right (no. 69) with its glass-covered terraces to left and right of the entrance.

We arrived at one o'clock, quite hungry after a long drive, and quite lucky to find a table still available in the small, lively dining room. Sometimes they prepare a *brandade* here, and I hoped that they might have it since I had recently made this rather laborious Provençal dish (based on dried cod, garlic, olive oil and milk) at home, carefully following an authentic recipe, and wanted to compare "the real thing". But today, a Friday, *truite au citron* (trout) was the main course on the menu (consisting of an entrée and a main dish, the entrée being, for example, a mixed salad or avocado with spicy mayonnaise). The price, which includes a quarter of a litre of red *vin du Gard* or a bottle of beer or mineral water, is 59F, only 5F higher than in 1984! — a remarkably small rise in price, matched by an unchanged level of quality and abundance.

My companion opted for the *brioche de poisson*, a small, crisp, slightly sweetened roll filled with mixed seafood and served with a well-flavoured herb sauce. My *salade de viande* consisted of a generous helping of various kinds of meat and sausages, cut into small cubes, served on a bed of crisp curly endive and seasoned with a vinaigrette that seemed a little vinegary to me. The trout was large, a little flabby but quite tasty, and accompanied by steamed potatoes. This light meal was well complemented by a rather curious dry Bordeaux rosé called *vin gris de Radegonde* for 80F. A fresh, light, agreeably sharp wine matching both the food and our thirst admirably. The house wine, a *vin du Gard* offered with the menu, comes from the southern Rhône valley and can be ordered by the half-litre carafe in white, rosé or red for 38F.

The wine list offers quite a good selection of clarets with some nine *grands crus classés* among them (500 to 900F) plus such *bourgeois* growths as a 1982 Château Chasse-Spleen (what's in a name?) for 350F. Perhaps a wine suitable for dinner, when there is no fixed-price menu, and the bill of fare offers such dishes as *magret de canard à l'aigre doux* (breast of duck with a sweet-sour sauce) for 85F. Other possibilities: *pavé de rumsteack au roquefort* (75F), *canard à l'orange* (80F), *sauté d'agneau aux haricots* (lamb with beans) for 75F. The *jambonette de volailles à l'estragon* is a speciality of the cook: a boned chicken leg stuffed with a tarragon filling, at 75F. And of course, there are a number of fish dishes including an interesting *choucroute de poissons* (fish sauerkraut) (90F).

The choice of wine is not limited to claret or the three or four burgundies listed (disproportionately overpriced by the shippers). There is also a quite attractively well-flavoured Côtes-du-Frontonnais (A.O.C.): Château Bellevue-la-Fôret for 70F a bottle, also available in half-bottles at exactly half the price.

Apart from the customary cheese course (28F), there are eight desserts listed, all of which are *"fait maison"* (home-made) for 32F. Willem chose *pithiviers chaud aux amandes*, warm puff pastry filled with almond and rum flavoured cream (a regional speciality from the Orléans region), while I enjoyed a *charlotte aux mandarines*, an airy mousse of mandarines in a *crème anglaise* (custard). The *charlotte* is said to have been created at the end of the eighteenth century in honour of George III's queen, Charlotte.

The coffee is good at 10F (don't expect to be served a second or third cup "on the house" here, or anywhere in Paris — or in the whole of France for that matter. Of course, you can get another cup on request, but it will be put on the bill). The service is attentive and prompt, the atmosphere is bustling, the clientèle mixed: older people, young people . . . but they all have one thing in common: they are manifestly content. So are we!

Open: *Orders taken until 10 pm*
Closed: *Sunday and Monday*
Métro: *12 Lamarck Caulaincourt*   **Map:** *8*
Approximate price: *140F*

Aux Négociants
27 rue Lambert
Tel: 46 06 15 11

A misleading name for this honest place which certainly does not sell merchant (*négociant*) blends, but authentic wines bought directly from the growers and partly bottled by the *patron*, Jean Navier, as befits a genuine wine bistro.

Here we are on the "good" side of the hill of Montmartre, on its still unmistakably Parisian slope, hardly contaminated by the kind of commercialism and mass tourism that has made the other side so vulgar and expensive. This is the side where you still find places such as **Le Maquis** (see p.159) and **Le Clodenis** (57, rue Caulaincourt, tel: 46.06.20.26), its chic twin brother.

Viewed from the rue Custine, the light blue façade of **Aux Négociants** immediately catches the eye along with the white sign with name in blue letters. It opens around midday as the friendly sales girl in the newspaper shop next door told me when I hesitated in front of the closed shutters of **Aux Négociants** at about a quarter to twelve.

Once inside, my attention is absorbed by the wines listed on a board above the horsehoe-shaped *zinc*. There are seven white wines on offer per glass (7cl): a 1987 Jasnières, very aromatic and very typical for the *appellation* with an elegantly pronounced acidity at 6.50F a glass. The area of this *appellation*, about halfway between Tours and Le Mans, covers only about ten hectares, which is equivalent to less than two and a half acres. The Savennières 1987, another little known Loire *appellation* originates from Château d'Epiré, and is very direct and full bodied (8F). Then there is a 1987 Montlouis (produced by Leblois – 6.50F) the left-bank relation of the better known, and generally more expensive, Vouvray, and a mellow 1987 Coteaux-du-Layon with a complex acidic background flavour from Leduc at Faye d'Anjou for 8.50F. So far, all these wines are from the Loire valley and made from the Chenin grape. In addition, there is a Valançay by Jacky Preys (5F) which is simple and good. It also comes from the Loire but its grape is Sauvignon blended with other local grapes. Very seldom found in a wine bistro is the Alsatian Sylvaner of which the 1986 vintage costs 6.50F here.

The emphasis on white Loire wines, with the rare Jasnières at the top of the list, reflects the preference of the owner, and to my knowledge this is the only wine bistro in Paris where you can sample this distinctive wine by the glass. Five red wines are available by the glass for between 5F and 9F; Bourgueil, Anjou Gamay, Anjou from the Cabernet Franc grape, Saumur-Champigny and – again an outsider – Carianne, a Rhône wine.

Every weekday (not on Saturday) around one o'clock, a hot meal is served to a mixed clientèle, consisting mainly of enthusiastic regulars at some six or eight tables covered with light blue formica. The repertoire announced for each day of a given week can look like this: Monday – *andouillette au jasnières* (chitterling sausage cooked in Jasnières), Tuesday – *épaule de boeuf* (shoulder of beef), Wednesday – *choux farci* (stuffed cabbage), Thursday – *épaule d'agneau aux petits légumes* (shoulder of lamb with vegetables), Friday – *haddock poché*. These dishes cost about 50F and can be preceded by *rillettes de canard* (minced duck simmered slowly in its own fat) or a chicken liver terrine, both at 28F, while sliced sausage from the Landes region is available at 20F. Cheeses comprise *bleu d'Auvergne*, *Pont l'Évêque*, *chèvre fermier* (farmhouse goat's cheese) and cost between 18 and 22F. A cheese tart is sometimes on offer for 20F but there can also be a strawberry tart in season. Be sure to order your fruit tart at the beginning of the meal or you may miss out – which would be a pity because the pastry is home-made and uncommonly delicious.

With your meal you may want to have a good bottle of red wine, or continue with wine by the glass. Of course, all the wines offered by the glass are also available by the bottle at ten times the price. Then there is a very recommendable 1988 Anjou *rouge* Clos de Médecin for 80F, and a 1988 Saint-Pourçain, a Gamay wine from the Auvergne region for 60F. A good young Coteaux-du-Loir for 55F, very popular here, comes from a region just south west of the small Jasnières area and is made of Cabernet, Gamay and Pineau d'Aunis by the grower Gaston Cartereau at Lhomme. This wine is a model of a light, refreshing red and is best drunk *"bien frais"*, well below room temperature. A host of other red wines includes a 1988 Chinon from the wine grower Dozon, Cuvée des Fabrices, at 75F and a 1985 Pécharmant at 90F, a Dordogne wine which is perhaps more suited to the colder months and best opened about half an hour before you want to drink it. It is especially good with a hearty cheese.

The *rillettes* come in an earthenware vessel together with a pot of gherkins with wooden pincers. You serve yourself with as much as you want and let the waiter take away the remainder. If you are very hungry there may be no remainder, as – to my utter surprise – was the case with two gentlemen at a neighbouring table who finished all the *rillettes* and who still managed to eat their enormous rolls of stuffed cabbage, with generous slices of fried bacon on top of them! But then the stuffed cabbage was very tasty!

The atmosphere is relaxed and very informal. During the mealtime, Jean Navier, the blond young *patron* kept his place behind the light blue formica-covered *zinc* pouring wine for a group of people including a smartly dressed gentleman standing in between a construction worker in a blue overall and an artistic-looking young man with a large beard. Only once in a while Jean leaves the bar to show someone to a table.

During the summer you may expect some lighter main dishes such as *coq au vin du deuxième jour*, a chicken casserole in red wine prepared one day in advance, which enhances the flavour.

If you want to acquaint yourself with the daily goings-on in a thoroughly Parisian wine bistro that serves unusual wines and wholesome family dishes, then **Aux Négociants** over the Montmartre hill is the place. Be there early to get a table (and a pastry) and to enjoy a few white Loire wines as an aperitif at the *zinc*.

Open: *12 to 7 pm* . *Tuesday, Thursday and Friday: 12 to 10 pm*
Closed: *Saturday and Sunday*
Métro: *4 Château Rouge or 12 Lamarck Coulaincourt   Map 8*
Approximate price: *150F*

Porte de Montreuil, Belleville, Pere Lachaise

Arrondissement 20

Au Boeuf Gros Sel
120 rue des Grands-Champs
Tel: 43.73.96.58

A warm sunny spring day around noon, a low building on the corner of a small, quiet leafy street, a man standing comfortably by his front door with a little dog playing at his feet: the components of an idyllic scene which makes you think you are in a sleepy French village rather than in the twentieth *arrondissement* of Paris. The impression is not destroyed when you enter, via the anteroom and bar, the clean, sunny dining room with its timber-framed walls. Plastic red and white check tablecloths cover the nine or ten small tables which accommodate no more than twenty-five people.

You don't have to worry about what to order here as there is no written menu. The *patronne* will put down a bottle of Beaujolais on your table as a sort of welcome gesture (you only pay for what you drink) and quietly proceed serving the *hors d'oeuvre*: three earthenware terrines to begin with: a fine chicken liver mousse, a coarse *terrine* and a pot of succulent *rillettes* (minced pork cooked in its own fat). Good gherkins and a supply of French bread come with the terrines.

Next come three large bowls of salad: lentils with onion in a mustard mayonnaise, celeriac with *sauce rémoulade*, and diced beetroot. As with the terrines, you take as much as you want, keeping in mind that the main course will be equally delicious and copious, and that there are other *hors d'oeuvre* to come yet: a salad of boiled beef, one of cold black pudding with onions, and one of potatoes with mayonnaise, all of them delicious, tasty and wholesome. The potato salad especially is a minor masterpiece.

The finale to this course is a bowl of solid salt herring fillets in their marinade of vegetable oil, onions and carrots.

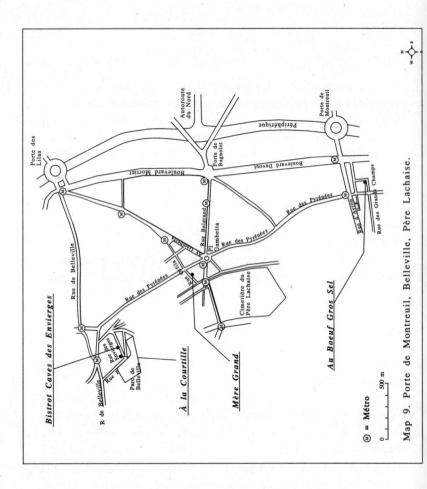

Map 9. Porte de Montreuil, Belleville, Père Lachaise.

What a treat! Two middle-aged gentlemen who have arrived in the meantime and have taken a table in the corner of the cosy dining room are obviously also enjoying this outstanding example of *"la vraie cuisine française"*.

The main course from which the bistro has taken its name, finally arrives at the table on a large plate: two whole carrots, a heap of cooked leeks, two large boiled potatoes, and several different cuts of boiled beef, each one more sumptuous than the last. As to the quantity: impossible for one person to eat it all. So much for the beef. The *gros sel* (coarse salt) has been present on the table all the time in a small glass bowl . . . as well as some mustard, spicy but not too sharp, in one of those little yellow pots.

It seems a miracle that, after such a long series of delicious dishes (eleven up to now, according to my count), there is now one which almost outdoes the preceding ones: a very generous portion of soft cheese on a wooden board which turns out to be the best Brie that I have ever tasted.

A complete meal in a genuine French restaurant is not finished with the cheese. A delicious piece of warm apple pie concludes the feast, and even the bill, 215F including a cup of coffee, leaves no bitter aftertaste.

Jean-Pierre Imbach originally wrote about this place in his *Paris Gourmand* as early as 1980. Nothing has changed in the past ten years except the prices, of course. And that is very fortunate, except for one little detail: Jean-Pierre had euphemistically described the house Beaujolais as *"pas terrible"* and I found it rather mediocre myself. At 90F a bottle, there are so many better wines worthy of accompanying such a divine meal!

Closed: *Saturday and Sunday*
Métro: *9 Maraîchers*   **Map:** *9*
Approximate price: *170F*

A La Courtille
1 rue des Envièrges
Tel: 46.36.51.59

It has taken quite some time for this restaurant to open its doors. Finally on 14th November 1990 the public was admitted. Bernard Pontonnier, its co-owner, and *"spiritus rector"* so to speak, talked to me about it at least three years before when he knew that his contract as director of a chic wine bar in the heart of the super-chic eighth *arrondissement* near the Champs Elysées would soon expire. In the meantime, that bistro has itself expired while Bernard Pontonnier has just begun to flourish again at **A la Courtille** on top of a hill far above the Elysian Fields.

Who is Bernard Pontonnier?

At his original location, the then famous **Cafe de la Nouvelle Mairie** near the Panthéon, he won the Académie Rabelais' *Coupe du Meilleur Pot* award as early as 1982. I "discovered" this quintessential wine bistro about 1981 and immediately fell in love with it for the unique blend of knowledgeable seriousness and benevolent irony with which the establishment's *raison d'être*, Wine with a capital W, was treated by the *patron* and the numerous dedicated wine-lovers who crowded the small area around the *zinc* from morning to night. That discovery was also my first real chance to appreciate the unique phenomenon which is the Paris wine bistro.

The basic elements – good wine from carefully selected growers and delicate *charcuterie*, cheese and bread from small, skilful artisans – make for communal enjoyment, shared appreciation of the ingenuity and dedication of their makers, and understanding of the *patron*'s pride in having discovered them and the people behind them – farmers, *charcutiers*, cheesemakers, and wine-growers.

What is Bernard Pontonnier's new restaurant like?

It is larger than his first tiny wine bistro. About eighty can be seated in an oblong dining area, with large picture windows, screened by Venetian blinds at night, looking out over the city skyline down below; and in a more cosy, rectangular space in the back. The counter with a large, built-in bowl of ice water for keeping wine bottles cool, is to the left of the entrance and overlooks both parts of the dining room.

Dining areas in a wine bistro? Well, if this new place has a lot in common with a wine bistro, it also has some of the characteristics of a *brasserie*: its opening hours (from 11 am to 1 am continuously); the draught beer on demand; and the simple, sober décor and service. Tables are always set with plates, knives, forks, wine glasses, and large linen napkins on paper-covered linen tablecloths. So it is obvious that they are not meant to be occupied just for a glass of wine, beer, orange juice with water *(orange pressée)*, or coffee.

Practically all twenty-odd wines listed on one page of the handwritten bill of fare are available by the glass which will be filled at the table by the *patron* or a young waiter clad in white apron, white dress shirt, black waistcoat and bow tie. The availability of a variety of wines by the glass is a distinct wine bistro feature, while the waiter's attire is more typical for a *brasserie*. When looking more closely at the wine list, I discovered that the wines on offer all come directly from small individual growers. You may question the choice of wines available but the care and good judgement applied in making the selection are apparent and undeniable. Five whites from five different growers in three different regions (Touraine, Alsace, and Rhône) and seventeen reds from fourteen growers in seven regions. No *rosé,* no sparkling wine. But when I arrived, the very first thing I was offered was a *flute* of sparkling wine which turned out to be a slightly sweet, agreeably aromatic Gaillac *mousseux* made according to a natural procedure which is older and perhaps more difficult to master than the *méthode champenoise*. This procedure, called *méthode gaillacoise*, includes a second fermentation in the bottle without the additon of any extra sugar.

On my first evening at **A la Courtille**, less than a month after it had opened, I took advantage of the late opening hours (orders for the kitchen are taken until 11.30 pm) arriving around half past nine after a rather tiring but pleasant day in the Touraine vineyards, and looking forward to having a few hours over a good meal with interesting wines. I was glad not to have arrived later (I had neglected to book) because within an hour the dining room had filled up and groups of people were waiting for tables while sipping glasses of Gaillac *mousseux*.

There is a wide choice from six entrées (30F), five main dishes (65 and 70F), two or three cheeses (25F), and four desserts (30F) offered on the bill of fare. There is also to be a different *plat du jour* every day at lunchtime.

Passing over the two mussel dishes (one of which is spiced with *colombo*, a milder spice variant of curry much in use in the French West Indies and containing garlic, coriander, turmeric, Jamaica hot peppers, saffron, cinnamon, and dried mango pulp); the duck terrine with preserved cabbage *(choux confits)*; the potted rabbit in jelly *(hure de lapin)* with *tapenade* (a paste of olive oil, black olivers, capers and anchovy) or the small Channel mackerel *(lisettes)* with shellfish, I ordered the *éffiloché de queue de boeuf*, boiled boned oxtail with onion rings and chives in a deliciously tasty vinaigrette, served agreeably tepid with French bread.

While taking sips from a glass of white 1989 Cheverny Chardonnay (from the growers Puzelat et Fils at Montils in the north-eastern part of Touraine), I admired the black and white photographs of Paris on the walls. The Cheverny is light and refreshing and has the characteristic taste of the Chardonnay grape (also used to make great white Burgundy where, however, frequently its specific flavours are overpowered by an excess of vanilla from the oak casks in which they have matured). Like all other wines here, it is poured from a bottle on which the grower's label has been replaced by **A la Courtille**'s own label giving the grower's name and address underneath the wine's *appellation*.

My main dish, two large potatoes in their jackets, filled with cod browned in the oven, served in a small puddle of sauce, has a very pronounced flavour due to judicious spicing. I drank two glasses of red 1988 Touraine Côt from the growers Cadart et Fils at Meusnes with this ample dish. The cool, dark red, concentrated wine with the typical flavour of the Côt grape (sometimes also called Malbec) distinctly marked by the soil on which the vines grow, proved a good companion to the hearty dish. It cost the same as the Cheverny: 11F a glass and 65F a bottle. Other reds on offer, somewhat surprisingly, include as many as five wines from the Beaujolais district for between 80F (1990 and 1989 Beaujolais and

1990 Beaujolais-Villages), and 130F (1989 Morgon *vieilles vignes* — from old vines, and 1989 Brouilly). Then, of course, there are seven reds from the Loire valley (from which Bernard Pontonnier also originates: *millésime* 1947, a very good vintage year!). They include two very interesting Gamays (1989 and 1990) from the young grower and wine-maker Charles Guerbois at Chémery in Touraine at 65F a bottle, a 1989 Chinon and a Bourgeuil from the same vintage year for 100F each and two red Anjou wines at 75F and 90F. Two Rhône wines (75F and 110F), a red 1989 Gaillac from grower Alain Rotier (75F) complete the list of identifiable growths. The other two reds on the list are less known to me: a 1989 Coteaux-de-Bessilles "Bronzinelle" made by François Henry for 65F, and a wine which apparently has no right to any *appellation*, being simply listed as *vin de table de France*, French table wine, but with a vintage year (1989), the name Thierry Allemand, and the surprisingly high price (for a simple *vin de table*) of 90F.

My dessert was *pain perdu crème anglaise,* pieces of French bread, soaked in milk together with beaten egg, almond slivers, raisins, and wafer-thin slices of baked apple, floating in a vanilla custard, a time-honoured French dessert that I had never before encountered in a restaurant. Other options are *crème brulée* (cold cream-based custard with caramel topping), a crisp thin pancake *(galette croustillante)* with exotic fruit and something called *suprème de chocolat parfumé au café.*

I had asked for a glass of young, mellow Coteaux-du-Layon to go with my dessert, but to his regret Bernard Pontonnier had to admit that they did not have any liqueurs at the moment, only to reappear after a few minutes with a glass of cool, delicious Coteaux-du-Layon which he seemed to have magically obtained from God knows where. A cup of good strong espresso coffee at a mere 7F concluded my meal which came to 170F altogether, not including the Coteaux-du-Layon, offered as a gift by the *patron.*

Undeniably, Bernard Pontonnier (together with François Morel, owner of the adjacent **Bistrot-Cave des Envierges**) has realised to the full his original idea of "a rigorously contemporary décor in an establishment where everything is spinning around Wine like the planets around the sun" which he had enthusiastically described as early as 1987. **A La Courtille** defies classification and cannot be placed within any specific fashion trend in Paris, or anywhere else, for that matter. But you do get more than excellent value for money: you can profit from the outstanding inventiveness and taste of Bernard Pontonnier, his associate and his cook. The latter's delicious vinaigrette brought back memories of a meal I had had at their former bistro three years before, where he had also officiated in the kitchen.

Open: *Seven days a week from 11 am to 1 am*
Métro: *11 Pyrénées*   **Map:** *9*
Approximate price: 185F

Bistrot-Cave des Envierges
11 rue des Envierges
Tel: 46.36.47.84

This small neighbourhood wine bistro is now a bit overshadowed by the recently opened **A la Courtille** (page 168) a few yards up the same street. Its owner, François Morel, now divides his time between these two establishments while his cook, the good-humoured and food-loving Nadine, now divides her time between the kitchen where she prepares succulent terrines and original hot dishes, and the small bar with its convivial wood-covered *zinc*.

Nadine's recipes include a *pistache de Saint-Gaudens*, a stew of shoulder of lamb and pork with white haricot beans and a good measure of garlic, a regional favourite from the Languedoc which I thoroughly enjoyed on one of my first visits; together with a bottle of good red Côtes-du-Roussillon from the Château de Jau at Cases-de-Pène near Rivesaltes.

Another one of her specialities is the *coq au vin à la façon de Madame Maigret* which goes back to an Alsatian recipe furnished by Georges Simenon. This chicken stew is cooked in dry white Alsatian Riesling wine, bound with egg yolk and *crème fraîche* (slightly soured cream) and enlivened at the last moment with some lemon juice and a small glass of *eau-de-vie de prunelle* (sloe spirit from Alsace). This dish is served with traditional noodles and best accompanied by a bottle of Riesling from the grower André Kientzler at Ribeauvillé.

Yet another curiosity-inspiring dish from Nadine's repertoire is *grillade de mariniers du Rhône* presumably made with fresh Rhône fish. I have not yet had the opportunity to try it, and perhaps you will beat me to it.

Hot dishes of this kind are available every day at midday and on Wednesday, Thursday, and Friday night. Make sure to book on Sundays because it is always crowded and the last guests leave around 5 pm. The price of the day's dish is around 45F. A plate of various cold cuts (*assiette de charcuterie*) or one of assorted cheeses is 38F while raw, cured, air-dried Bayonne ham is 20F, the same as air-dried sausage, a single cheese and a delicious *terrine de canard* (duck) served with preserved *griottes*, light-coloured, sour cherries which go very well with duck terrine.

Wines (five whites and five reds) are on offer in quantities of 8cl, 16cl, and 75cl in glasses, carafes and bottles for prices from 6F to 53F for the least expensive and up to about double that for the most expensive. They are not all French (there is a rather unbalanced and shallow Soave Classico from Italy among the whites) but the Sauvignon (white) and the Gamay (red) de Touraine from Charles Guerbois at Chémery (Domaine des Acacias) are deliciously aromatic and fresh and excellent value for money. Other good reds: three vintages of Chinon *vieilles vignes* (old vines) from grower Jean-Marie Dozon: 1985 for 95F, 1986 for 82F, and 1988 for 70F, available only by the bottle. (To take away: 50F, 42F and 36F, respectively.) The 1985 or 1986 Saumur-Champigny from grower Denis Duveau at Varrains (Domaine des Roches Neuves) at 86F the bottle (45F to take away) also offers excellent value for money and is perhaps one of the best Saumur-Champigny wines available in Paris.

This is also a good place to try various vintages of mellow white Coteaux-du-Layon Rochefort from grower Grosset Château at Rochefort. 1980, 1979, 1976, 1971 and 1970 are available for between 86F and 150F a bottle – 45F and 80F a half-bottle. Other growers in the same region are represented too: Fernand Moron at Saint-Lambert, Yves Leduc at Faye, Vincent Lecointre at Rablay. Vouvray (Didier Champvalon), Savennieres (Clos du

Papillon, Soulez) and several Madirans (from Châteaux Bouscassé and Montus) are available as well.

Lovers of malt whisky, old Calvados and other rare liqueurs can also find their heart's content at **Envierges**: Glengarioch, Glendullan, Springbank, and Bowmore are available at 15F for 2 cl, while an eight-year-old Calvados Pays d'Auge is 18F, and prune liqueur Sainte-Catherine and *marc d'Irouleguy* (distilled from the grape residues of the rare Irouleguy wine from the eastern slopes of the Pyrenees) are 16F.

Open: *12.30 to 8.00 pm. Wednesday, Thursday and Friday 12.30 pm to 1 am*
Closed: *Monday and Tuesday*
Métro: *11 Pyrénées*   **Map:** *9*
Approximate price: *90F*

Mère-Grand
20 rue Orfila
Tel: 46.36.03.29

Why not have your midday meal in a small, authentic French restaurant right behind the Père-Lachaise cemetery? Especially if it is unpretentious and inexpensive.

The fixed-price menu at 55F starts with a rabbit pâté (*pâté de lapin*), perhaps a bit too compact but well-flavoured. One of the other two options for entrée, the leek tart (*tarte aux poireaux*) looked and smelled very attractive, but I noticed it too late. For the not very hungry, there are always *crudités*, a small dish of grated carrots and other raw vegetables.

Instead of the *coq au vin purée* (chicken in red wine with bacon, onions and mushrooms, served with mashed potatoes), I took the *tripoux d'Auvergne*, two small cushions of stuffed and spiced mutton tripe with four or five small potatoes sprinkled with fresh parsley. The tripe cushions (*tripoux*), a speciality from central France, can also be bought in tins at most grocery stores in Paris. If you don't like tripe you can have the *steak grillé*, the third menu option, which that day was served with spinach.

For dessert I had the choice between *mousse au chocolat, crème caramel,* and fruit cake (apricot or kiwi). The apricot cake was made of a good, crisply-baked dough and tasty apricot filling. The menu includes a quarter of a litre of mineral water, beer or wine. I chose the red house wine served in a 25cl carafe, and found it drinkable (you can dilute it with water, as a lot of French people do at midday – there is a carafe of fresh water on every table at **Mère-Grand**). The other red wines here are bottled by *négociants* (dealers) and stored in a special brick structure in the dining room – not the ideal place to store wine, so I advise you to abstain. There is also excellent Pelforth beer from northern France at 18F a bottle.

This little place is unpretentiously decorated with lace curtains on brass rods and old-fashioned, rather elaborate porcelain lamps hanging from the whitewashed ceiling. A bouquet of fresh flowers on a central table near the entrance and two large mirrors in carved wood frames complement well the prevailing mauve colour scheme on walls, tablecloths and napkins.

There were not many people there on the sunny spring afternoon that I took my meal at **Mère-Grand**, except regulars who were greeted with a friendly handshake by the dark-haired *patronne* who was assisted by one waitress with the *patron* behind the bar.

If you want to skip the entrée and the beverage included in the menu price, you can have the main course and dessert for 43F and your modest meal will come to 68F including a bottle of Pelforth beer and a cup of coffee. Of course, you may want to try the *confit de canard maison* (home-preserved duck – 70F) or a classic such as *canard à l'orange* (70F), or *blanquette d'agneau à l'estragon* (creamy lamb stew with tarragon – 65F). There is also a 105F three-course menu which is served at dinner, while the 55F menu, more elaborately served, costs 75F in the evenings.

Open: *12 to 2.30 pm and 7.30 to 9.30 pm*
Closed: *Sunday all day and Monday night*
Métro: *3 Gambetta, exit: place Martin-Nadaud* ***Map:*** *9*
Approximate price: *85F*
No reservations

Restaurants In Alphabetical Order

Restaurant names beginning with A (la), Au(x), La, Le(s), Chez, Auberge, Bistrot (la, le(s), de(s), du), Restaurant, Relais or Cave, are listed under the first letter of the following word in the name. (W) indicates a wine bistro.

Name	Arr.	Map No.	Page
Bistrot d'André	15	6	121
Chez Aristide	17	7	143
Astier	11	5	101
Au Babylone	7	3	57
Le Relais Beaujolais (W)	9	4	83
Le Beaujolais Cler (W)	7	3	58
Le Berthoud	5	2	29
Le Restaurant Bleu	14	6	124
Au Boeuf Gros Sel	20	9	165
A la Bonne Cuisine	17	7	145
Le Bougainville	2	1	11
Le Bourbonnais	14	6	126
Chartier	9	4	87
Le Château Poivre	14	6	128
Le Chevert (Auberge Comtoise)	7	3	60
A la Cloche des Halles (W)	1	1	13
A la Courtille (W)	20	9	168
Aux Crus de Bourgogne	2	1	15
La Cave Drouot (W)	9	4	89
Au Duc de Richelieu (W)	2	1	17
Bistrot-Cave des Envierges (W)	20	9	172
Aux Fins Gourmets	7	3	63
Chez Gaston (W)	4	5	103
Chez Germaine	7	3	65
Au Gourmet de l'Isle	4	2	53
La Grosse Tartine	17	7	148
Jenny Jacquet	Neuilly	7	151

Name	Arr.	Map No.	Page
Chez Léon (Le Rubis) (W)	1	1	19
Restaurant du Luxembourg	6	2	32
Ma Bourgogne (W)	8	7	155
Bistrot Le Mâconnais (W)	7	3	67
Le Maquis	18	8	159
Chez Marcel (Restaurant Antoine)	12	5	97
Jacques Mélac – Bistrot à Vins (W)	11	5	104
Mère Grand	20	9	174
Moissonnier	5	2	34
Monsieur Lapin	14	6	130
Aux Négociants (W)	18	8	161
Au Père Tranquille (W)	15	6	132
Restaurant Perraudin	5	2	37
Le Petit Mâchon	15	6	135
Le Petit Niçois	7	3	70
Aux Petits Oignons	7	3	75
Au Petit Tonneau	7	3	76
Au Pied de Fouet	7	3	79
Restaurant Polidor	6	2	39
Chex René	5	2	51
Chez Robert	4	5	107
Le Ruban Bleu	1	1	22
Runtz	2	1	24
Au Soleil d'Austerlitz (W)	5	2	42
Aux Tables de la Fontaine	11	5	111
Terminus Nord	10	4	91
Thé des Brumes	5	2	44
Le Tiburce	6	2	46
Chex Toutoune	5	2	48
Le Train Bleu	12	5	113
Le Traversière	12	5	117
Restaurant La Vézère	10	4	94
Au Vin des Rues (W)	14	6	137
Au Volcan	4	5	119

Restaurants and Wine Bistros (w) by Price

Less than 100F	Page
Au Babylone (85F)	57
Le Beaujolais Cler (w) (45F)	58
Le Bougainville (80F)	11
Chartier (75F)	87
A la Cloche des Halles (w) (75F)	13
Bistrot–Cave des Envierges (w) (90F)	172
Chez Gaston (w) (95F)	103
Chez Germaine (60F)	65
Chez Léon (w) (90F)	19
Jacques Mélac – Bistrot à Vins (w) (85F)	104
Mère Grand (85F)	174
Thé des Brumes (95F)	44

100F to 150F	
Bistrot d'André (145F)	121
A la Bonne Cuisine (110F)	145
Le Chevert (110F)	60
Restaurant du Luxembourg (120F)	32
Le Maquis (140F)	159
Aux Négociants (W) (150F)	161
Restaurant Perraudin (145F)	37
Aux Petits Oignons (150F)	75
Au Pied de Fouet (115F)	79
Restaurant Polidor (135F)	39
Au Vin des Rues (W) (140F)	137
Au Volcan (45F)	119

160F to 200F	
Astier (180F)	101
Au Boeuf Gros Sel (170F)	165
Le Château Poivre (180F)	128
A la Courtille (W) (185F)	168
Au Duc de Richelieu (W) (160F)	17
Aux Fins Gourmets (190F)	63
Au Gourmet de l'Isle (160F)	53
Ma Bourgogne (W) (185F)	155

Restaurants Open Late / Sundays

Until 10 pm

Chez Léon (except on Saturday)	19
Aux Tables de la Fontaine	111
Aux Négociants (Tuesday, Thursday & Friday only)	161
Le Maquis	159
Au Vin des Rues	137
Thé des Brumes (except on Saturday)	44
Le Train Bleu	113

Until 10.15 pm

Le Tiburce	46
Chez René	51

Until 10.30 pm

Jacques Mélac (Tuesday & Thursday only)	104
Bistrot le Mâconnais	67

Until 11 pm

Aux Crus de Bourgogne (for *foie gras* and *langouste* only)	15

Until midnight

Runtz	24
Chez Gaston	103

After midnight

Terminus Nord (until 0.30 am)	91
Le Berthoud (until 1 am)	29
Polidor (until 1am – except on Sunday)	39
A la Courtille (until 1 am)	168
Bistrot-Cave des Envierges (until 1 am on Wednesday, Thursday & Friday)	172
Au Duc de Richelieu (until 5 am)	17

Restaurants Open on Sunday

4th *arrondissement*:	Au Gourmet de l'Isle
5th *arrondissement* :	Moissonnier (for lunch only)
6th *arrondissement*:	Restaurant Polidor
7th *arrondissement*:	Le Beaujolais Cler (until 3 pm)
9th *arrondissement*:	Chartier
10th *arrondissement*:	Terminus Nord
12th *arrondissement*:	Le Traversière
	Le Train Bleu
14th *arrondissement*:	Monsieur Lapin
17th *arrondissement*:	La Grosse Tartine
20th *arrondissement*:	A La Courtille
	Bistrot-Cave des Envièrges

Favourite Sunday Lunch Restaurants

	Page
Moisonnier	34
Le Traversière	117
Monsieur Lapin	130
A La Courtille	168
Bistrot-Cave des Envierges	172
La Grosse Tartine	148

Restaurants along the Métro Lines

Métro. No.	Stations	Restaurants
1	**Pont de Neuilly – Château de Vincennes**	
	Porte Maillot:	Jenny Jacquet
		La Grosse Tartine
	Tuilleries:	Chez Léon
	Louvre:	A la Cloche des Halles
	Hôtel de Ville:	Chez Gaston
		Au Volcan
	Saint-Paul:	Chez Robert
	Bastille:	Chez Robert
	Gare de Lyon:	Le Train Bleu
		Le Traversière
2	**Porte Dauphine – Nation**	
	Rome:	Chez Aristide
	Villiers:	Chez Aristide
	Place de Clichy:	A La Bonne Cuisine
	Colonel-Fabien:	La Vézère
3	**Pont de Levallois – Gallieni**	
	Villiers:	Chez Aristide
	Quatre-Septembre:	Runtz
	Bourse:	Le Bougainville
	Sentiers:	Aux Crus de Bourgogne
	Parmentier:	Astier
		Aux Tables de la Fontaine
	Gambetta:	Mère Grand
4	**Porte de Clignancourt – Porte d'Orléans**	
	Château-Rouge:	Aux Négociants
	Gare du Nord:	Terminus Nord
	Les Halles:	Aux Crus de Bourgogne
	Odéon	Polidor
	Saint-Sulpice:	Le Tiburce

Saint-Placide:	Restaurant du Luxembourg
Montparnasse-Bienvenue	Au Père Tranquille
Vavin:	Le Bourbonnais
Denfert-Rochereau:	Au Vin des Rues

5   Église de Pantin – Place d'Italie:

Gare d'Austerlitz:	Au Soleil d'Austerlitz
Bastille:	Chez Robert
Gare du Nord:	Terminus Nord

6   Charles de Gaulle Étoile – Nation

Montparnasse-Bienvenue	Au Père Tranquille
Edgar-Quinet:	Le Bourbonnais
Denfert-Rochereau:	Au Vin des Rues

7   Fort d'Aubervilliers – Mairie d'Ivry

Pyramides:	Le Bougainville
	Chez Léon
	Le Ruban Bleu
Châtelet:	Aux Crus de Bourgogne
Pont-Marie:	Au Gourmet de L'Isle
Jussieu:	Moissonnier

8   Créteil Préfecture – Balard

Ledru-Rollin:	Chez Marcel
	Le Traversière
Bastille:	Chez Robert
Rue Montmartre:	Chartier
Richelieu-Drouot:	Au Duc de Richelieu
	La Cave Drouot
Invalides:	Au Petit Tonneau
La Tour Maubourg:	Au Petit Tonneau
	Le Beaujolais Cler
	Le Petit Niçois
École Militaire:	Le Beaujolais Cler
	Le Chevert
Boucicaut:	Le Petit Mâchon
Balard:	Le Bistrot d'André

9 Pont de Sèvres – Mairie de Montreuil

Miromesnil:	Ma Bourgogne
Richelieu-Drouot:	Au Duc de Richelieu
	La Cave Drouot
Rue Montmartre:	Chartier
Charonne:	Jacques Mélac
Maraîchers:	Au Boeuf Gros Sel

10 Porte d'Auteuil – Gare d'Austerlitz

Duroc:	Chez Germaine
Vaneau:	Chez Germaine
	Au Pied de Fouet
Sèvres-Babylone:	Au Babylone
	Au Pied de Fouet
Maubert-Mutualité:	Chez Toutoune
	Le Berthoud
Cardinal-Lemoine:	Chez René
Jussieu:	Moissonnier
Gare d'Austerlitz:	Au Soleil d'Austerlitz

11 Châtelet – Mairie des Lilas

Châtelet:	Aux Crus de Bourgogne
Hôtel de Ville:	Chez Gaston
	Au Volcan
Rambuteau:	Chez Gaston
Pyrénées:	A La Courtille
	Bistrot-Cave des Envierges

12 Porte de la Chapelle – Mairie d'Issy

Lamark-Caulaincourt:	Le Maquis
	Aux Négociants
Notre-Dame-de-Lorette:	Le Relais Beaujolais
Solférino:	Aux Petits Oignons
Rue du Bac:	Aux Fins Gourmets
	Bistrot Le Mâconnais
Sèvres-Babylone:	Au Babylone
	Au Pied de Fouet

Notre-Dame-des-Champs Restaurant du Luxembourg
Montparnasse-Bienvenüe   Au Père Tranquille

13   Saint-Denis Basilique – Chatillon Montrouge

Place de Clichy: A La Bonne Cuisine
Miromesnil: Ma Bourgogne
Invalides: Au Petit Tonneau
Saint-François-Xavier: Au Petit Tonneau
Duroc: Chez Germaine
Montparnasse-Bienvenüe   Au Père Tranquille
Pernety: Monsieur Lapin
                           Le Restaurant Bleu
                           Le Château Poivre

RER B Gare du Nord – Dentfert – Rochereau

Gare du Nord: Terminus Nord
Les Halles: Aux Crus de Bourgogne
Luxembourg: Perraudin
Port Royal: Thé des Brumes
Denfert-Rochereau: Au Vin des Rues

[The RER B line — RER stands for *Réseau Exprès Régional* —
makes fewer stops and goes faster than the regular Métro lines.
Within the city limits of Paris, the regular Métro tickets are also
valid for the RER trains.]

Seventeen Wine Bistros and their Regional Wines by the Glass

Le Relais Beaujolais: Mâcon-Villages, Mâcon-Clessé, Beau-jolais- Villages, Brouilly, Chénas, Chiroubles, Juliénas, Saint-Amour, Moulin-à-Vent, Regnié, Saumur-Champigny, Chinon.

Le Beaujolais Cler: Cheverny-Sauvignon, Pouilly *fumé*, San-cerre, Cheverny-Gamay, Beaujolais, Saint-Amour.

A La Cloche Des Halles: Cheverny *blanc*, Bourgogne *blanc*, Mâcon *blanc*, Côte-de-Brouilly, Morgon, Chiroubles, Fleurie, Juliénas, Bourgueil.

A La Courtille: Gaillac *mousseux*, Cheverny-Chardonnay, Syl-vaner d'Alsace, Sauvignon de Touraine, Côtes-du-Rhône *blanc*, Klevner d'Alsace, Beaujolais, Beaujolais-Villages, Touraine Côt and Anjou *rouge*, Anjou-Villages, Bourgueil, Chinon, Côtes-du-Rhône, Gaillac *rouge*, Coteaux-de-Bessilles.

La Cave Drouot: Cheverny-Sauvignon, Quincy, Mâcon *blanc*, Pacherenc-de-Vic-Bilh, Madiran, Juliénas, Chénas, Morgon, Fleurie, Côte-de-Brouilly.

Au Duc de Richelieu: Muscadet, Muscadet de Sèvres-et-Maine *sur lie*, Beaujolais *blanc*, Fleurie, Regnié, Chiroubles, Ché-nas, Côtes-du-Rhône.

Bistrot-Cave des Envierges: Cheverny-Romorantin, Mont-louis *moelleux*, Vouvray *demi sec*, Sauvignon de Touraine, Gamey de Touraine, Bourgueil *vieilles vignes*, Minervois.

Chez Gaston: Cheverny, Mâcon *blanc*, Beaujolais, Côte-Roannaise, Côtes-du-Rhône-Villages-Beaumes-de-Venise, Corbières (Montagne d'Alaric).

Chez Léon: Côtes-du-Rhône *blanc*, Cheverny-Sauvignon, Mâcon-Clessé, Coteaux-du-Layon, Bourgueil, Chinon, Beaujolais, Côte-de-Brouilly, Fleurie, Moulin-à-Vent.

Ma Bourgogne: Mâcon-Clessé, Marsannay *rosé*, Gamay de Haut-Poitou, Beaujolais, Moulin-à-Vent and other Beaujolais growths.

Bistrot Le Mâconnais: Mâcon-Clessé, Môcon-Viré, Saint-Véran, Beaujolais *blanc*, Pouilly-Loché, Mâcon *rouge*, Beaujolais-Villages, Brouilly Chiroubles, Juliénas, Regnié.

Jacques Mélac – Bistrot à Vins: Chignin de Savoie, Sylvaner d'Alsace, Lirac *blanc*, Quincy, Màcon-Clessé, Vouvray *demi sec*, Jurançon *moelleux*, Gamay de Haut-Poitou, Coteaux-du-Lyonnais, Saint-Pourçain, Gamay de Touraine, Anjou *rouge*, Saumur-Champigny, Chinon, Beaujolais-Villages-Lantignié, Morgon, Saint-Joseph, Marcillac, Lirac *rouge*.

Aux Negociants: Jasnières, Savennières, Montlouis, Vouvray, Coteaux-du-Layon, Valancay blanc, Sylvaner d'Alsace, Anjou-Gamay, Anjou rouge, Saumur-Champigny, Bourgueil, Cairanne (Cotes-du- Rhone).

Au Père Tranquille: Saumur *blanc*, Saumur-Champigny, Chinon, Gamay de Touraine ...

Au Soleil d'Austerlitz: Bourgogne-Aligoté, Beaujolais *blanc*, Sauvignon de Touraine, Sancerre, Beaujolais *rosé*, Beaujolais-Villages, Côte-de-Brouilly, Morgon, Regnié, Juliénas, Chénas, Coteaux-du-Lyonnais, Anjou-Villages, Chinon (red and pink), Côtes-du-Frontonnais.

Au Vin des Rues: Clairette de Die, Crémant de Bourgogne, Bourgogne-Aligoté, Mâcon-Clessé, Côte-Roannaise, Coteaux-du-Lyonnais, Beaujolais, Beaujolais growths ...

Au Volcan: Quincy, Coteaux-d'Auvergne, Gamay de Touraine, Saint-Emilion, Sancerre.

Nine French Regions and their Gastronomic Embassies in Paris

Any division of France into gastronomic regions is inclined to be arbitrary. However, the following represent the local traditions usually recognised.

Alsace	Runtz, Terminus Nord
Loire	Jenny Jacquet, Le Traversière
Périgord	La Vézère
Auvergne and Bourbonnais	Le Restaurant Bleu, Jacques Mélac Le Bourbonnais
Lyonnais and Beaujolais	Moissonnier, Le Petit Mâchon, Chez René, Le Relais Beaujolais, Au Vin des Rues, Le Train Bleu
Bourgogne	Le Tiburce, Bistrot le Mâconnais Ma Bourgogne
Franche Comté (Jura)	Le Chevert, Moissonnier
Provence	Au Petit Niçois, Chez Toutoune

Your Co-operation will be Appreciated

When you discover an attractive establishment in Paris which you think worthy to be included in this guide, do let us know, and when you want to comment on or criticise a restaurant or bistro listed in this guide (pleasant surprises or sad disappointments) please do not hesitate to do so. Sometimes a change in ownership or a new chef will suffice to turn a good restaurant into a bad one. You can also fill in the attached form and send it (enclosing a business card of the restaurant concerned, if possible) to:

Gaston Wijnen, c/o Rosendale Press Ltd, Premier House, 10 Greycoat Place, London SW1

Readers who furnish relevant information that we use in the following edition, will be sent a free copy with the compliments of the publisher.

Thank you very much.

Restaurant . . . .

Telephone No. . . . .

No . . . . . Street . . . . Arr. . . . .

Closed . . . . Last orders taken before . . . . h

Ambience and décor . . . .

Welcome . . . .

Service . . . .

What you ate . . . .

. . . .

. . . .

The price of your meal . . . . F . . . . . .

The quality of the dishes . . . .

. . . .

House specialities . . . .

. . . .

. . . .

The wine list . . . .

. . . .

. . . .

Additional remarks . . . .

. . . .

Value for money: excellent-very good-good-adequate-poor

Restaurant visited on . . . . 19 . for lunch/dinner

By (your name and address) . . . .

. . . .